JOHN WAYNE

TREASURES

JOHN WAYNE

TREASURES

RANDY ROBERTS | DAVID WELKY

becker&mayer!
BOOK PRODUCERS

© 2012 by becker&mayer! LLC

Text copyright © 2012 by Randy Roberts and David Welky

This 2012 edition published by becker&mayer!

www.beckermayer.com

Note: All removable documents and memorabilia are reproductions of original items and are not originals themselves.

Design: Rosebud Eustance
Editorial: Amelia Riedler and Dana Youlin
Image Research: Jessica Eskelsen and Shayna Ian
Production: Tom Miller

ISBN 978-1-60380-271-0

Manufactured at Legend Color in Shatin, NT Hong Kong

2 4 6 8 10 9 7 5 3 1

frontispiece JOHN WAYNE IN *THE SEARCHERS*, 1956.

opposite YOUNG JOHN WAYNE IN *THE BIG TRAIL*, 1930.

pages 170–171 DUKE'S SET CHAIR, 1975

page 176 JOHN WAYNE POSING FOR *THE MAN WHO SHOT LIBERTY VALANCE*, 1962.

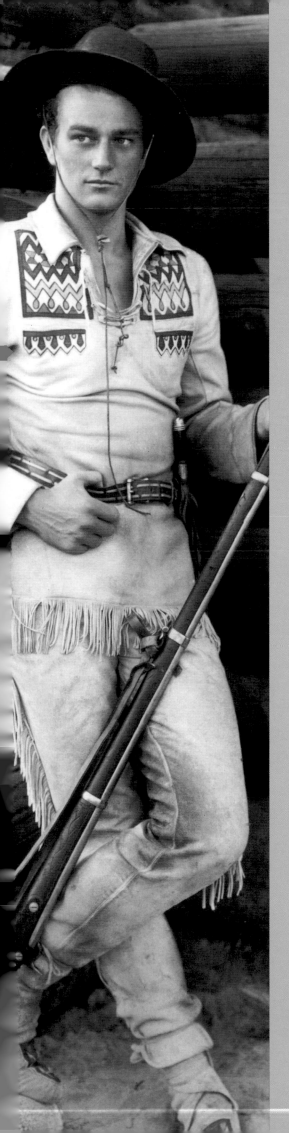

CONTENTS

MAKING JOHN WAYNE

"WELL, I SURE AS HELL WASN'T GOING TO NAME MY FIRSTBORN 'MARION'—ANY KID NAMED MARION'S GONNA HAVE A ROUGH RIDE AND I SHOULD KNOW."

John Wayne—his friends called him "Duke"—understood that his film roles created a persona that millions of fans revered. He also understood that he was not "John Wayne"—the image or the name. Yet he bore the title with pride, accepting the burden it carried with character, determination, and integrity.

"I never have become accustomed to the 'John,'" the man born Marion Morrison confessed. "Nobody even really calls me John. It's [just] a name that goes well together and it's like one word—John Wayne."

Being "John Wayne" brought grave responsibilities. Those two words stood for a way of life. For pride. Patriotism. Doing things the right way. Speaking your mind. Standing up for what was right.

⭐

opposite JOHN WAYNE IN HIS FIRST WESTERN, *THE BIG TRAIL*, 1930.

The lines separating private life from public image blurred as Marion Morrison incorporated elements of John Wayne's screen character into himself. Eventually until the thirty-foot giant on-screen became virtually indistinguishable from the six-foot-four-inch big cat of a man. President Jimmy Carter once called Wayne "a symbol of many of the qualities that made America great—the ruggedness, the tough independence, the sense of personal conviction and courage, on and off the screen—that reflected the best of our national character." Carter saw no difference between Wayne the star and Wayne the man. By 1979, the year he died, neither did Duke.

———————— ✪ ————————

As he would so many times in his life, Marion Morrison made an impressive entrance. He arrived, all thirteen pounds of him, on May 26, 1907. His mother, Molly, disliked him from the beginning. An angry, opinionated woman, she was convinced that the delivery of her firstborn had nearly killed her. Molly's sweet-tempered, ineffectual husband, Clyde, saw the shrieking bundle as his new best friend. Marion was someone to play football with, someone to teach, someone to talk to.

Their hometown of Winterset, Iowa, (now home to the John Wayne Birthplace Museum) could have been the model for a portrait of small-town America. Nestled atop a river bluff, it boasted straight, wide streets and a dignified limestone courthouse. Victorian mansions lined the best neighborhood, not that the Morrisons lived in the best part of town; Clyde's salary as a pharmacist covered the rent on a modest four-room home that never hosted the social elite.

Clyde always imagined that success was just around the corner. His futile quest for the brass ring caused him to drag Molly, Marion, and his younger son, Bobby, through a succession of homes and towns, including, in 1914, a desolate plot of land near Lancaster, California. Molly shook with rage as she stepped from the train to view her new home for the first time. With its two paved streets, lack of electricity, and blazing hot climate, Lancaster had nothing to offer a socially ambitious woman. She hated the three-room shack Clyde had built. Even seven-year-old Marion recognized his father's folly. "We were cut off from the world," he remembered. "A stranger visitin' from Iowa wouldn't have believed he was in the twentieth century." Clyde's experiment lasted only a few years. Broke and tired of farming the desert, he retreated to the Los Angeles suburb of Glendale to take yet another pharmacist job. The Morrisons had moved two thousand miles to find themselves in the same situation they were in when they left Iowa.

Molly's constant abuse of Clyde drove sensitive young Marion away from the house. He arose at 4:30 a.m. to deliver newspapers, took after-school jobs, joined the Boy Scouts, and hung out at the YMCA. At the local library he devoured heroic biographies of great Americans and plunged into Zane Grey's Western novels. He also fell in love with the movies. Four or five times a week he thrilled at the exploits of Douglas Fairbanks, William S. Hart, and Tom Mix. Like many kids his age, he imagined himself projected upon the silver screen. Glendale's vacant lots became "sets" for dramas performed with his friends. A wooden box played the role of a movie camera. Marion also frequented nearby Kalem Studios, watching the professionals crank real cameras. On lucky days, crews let him sit down to lunch with them.

"His looks alone would stop traffic," a classmate once said. For this and other reasons, Marion was a popular boy at school. An eager student who enrolled in college prep courses and captained the school debate team, he was also polite and well mannered, if wary of entering into serious relationships with girls. He preferred the company of male students, especially ones who kept their cool and weren't prone to the kind of arguing he dealt with at home. And even though he was a jock—a lineman

on Glendale High's powerful football team—he had no patience for bullies.

By high school he had even overcome his feminine name, a frequent target for neighborhood boys. The Morrisons had a pet Airedale named Duke who followed Marion to school every day, often sleeping at a fire station until his master passed by after school. The firemen took to calling Marion "Little Duke" or just plain "Duke." He reveled in the manly nickname and made sure that it stuck. "Just call me Duke," he began telling people.

Molly showed little interest in her son's future, but Clyde encouraged Duke to consider a career in law. His football prowess earned him a scholarship

---

⭐

above MARION MORRISON PRACTICING THE SQUINT THAT WOULD MAKE HIM FAMOUS WHILE SITTING WITH HIS YOUNGER BROTHER, ROBERT, CIRCA 1915. THEIR FATHER, CLYDE, HAD RECENTLY MOVED THE FAMILY FROM IOWA TO A BLEAK PATCH OF CALIFORNIA SCRUBLAND.

HIGH SCHOOL YEARBOOK

Excerpt from Duke's Glendale High senior yearbook, circa 1925. Duke was very active in extra curricular clubs, including football and the dance committee.

COLLEGE PHOTOGRAPH

Duke poses in his University of Southern California football uniform, circa 1930. A shoulder injury would soon end his gridiron career.

opposite FIFTEEN-YEAR-OLD MARION MORRISON (LEFT) CLOWNS AROUND WITH FRIEND, CIRCA 1922. ALTHOUGH GIRLS THOUGHT HIM HANDSOME, DUKE WAS ALWAYS MORE COMFORTABLE AROUND HIS MALE FRIENDS.

to the University of Southern California, where he enrolled in its pre-law program. A part-time job washing dishes and busing tables at the Sigma Chi house covered extra expenses. He also pledged Sigma Chi, meaning that the same men he served were supposed to view him as a fraternity brother. Duke thrived despite the awkwardness of the situation. He continued his solid academic work, dated attractive women, and played football. At six-foot-four and two hundred pounds, he cut a dashing figure at the raucous parties that made up a considerable portion of his college life. USC's football team even got invited to drink with Hollywood starlets such as Clara Bow, Joan Crawford, and Lina Basquette. "We had a good time," one of his teammates winked, "but it wasn't *that* exciting."

USC game tickets were so hard to come by that even Western star Tom Mix had trouble getting his hands on some. Coach Howard Jones offered to give the actor a box at the stadium if he hired some of his players to work at Fox Studios over the summer. Duke Morrison got one of the prized spots moving furniture around the Fox lot for thirty-five dollars a week.

Duke gave little thought to his status at the bottom of the Hollywood food chain. It was just a summer job, and he had bigger problems to deal with. After years of animosity, his parents had separated just before the end of the school year. Duke was embarrassed and ashamed. He avoided his parents, stayed away from home, and suffered long fits of moodiness.

At the end of the summer, Duke separated his right shoulder while bodysurfing. Coach Jones, having no need for a lineman with a bad wing, dropped him from the squad and terminated his scholarship. Jones's move, besides depriving Duke the social cachet accorded to football players, also cost him a free seat at the team's training table, where he ate the largest meal of the day—no small matter considering his tight budget.

His scholarship gone, Duke sulked around the Sigma Chi house, drank too much, and, in a moment of youthful rebellion, flirted with socialism. He also started dating Josephine Saenz, a dark-eyed beauty from an aristocratic Hispanic family. They were in many ways opposites. She was a socialite and he was a nobody. She was cultured and he was raw. She was a devout Catholic and he was a lapsed Protestant. Josephine's parents thought Duke was beneath their daughter. Josephine, however, appreciated his lack of pretense. Duke loved Josephine's dignity, her calm beauty, and her social connections. They dated whenever he had money in his pocket and decided to marry if Duke could ever afford it.

---

opposite DUKE STRIKES A LINEMAN'S STANCE. FOOTBALL OFFERED HIM AN ENTRÉE TO PARTIES, A CHANCE TO DRINK WITH HOLLYWOOD STARLETS, AND ONE DEPENDABLE MEAL A DAY. WAYNE ESSENTIALLY GAVE UP ON COLLEGE ONCE HE LOST HIS SCHOLARSHIP.

Duke returned to Fox in the summer of 1927 hoping to make enough money to finish his studies. "I had no ambition beyond becoming the best property man on the Fox lot," he laughed. Directors occasionally used the attractive furniture schlepper as an extra, or asked him to perform a stunt for a few extra bucks in his pay envelope. Once the camera stopped rolling, he returned to his duties as if nothing had happened. "I really had no intention of being an actor," Duke remembered, "I had no desire for it." His life changed, however, when he dared to dump director John Ford on his rear.

— ☆ —

John Ford wasn't exactly a liar, but he wasn't very good at telling the truth. Depending on his mood, he might tell you that he was born Sean Aloysius O'Fearna in the Irish town of Galway, or that his uncle Mike had fought at the Battle of Shiloh, or that he had once cowboyed in Arizona. Or he might clam up and tell you nothing at all. "He was the most secretive man I ever knew," remembered a friend. "He could be talkative and friendly one day, another day abusive."

After an unremarkable childhood in Portland, Maine, John followed his older brother, Francis—a well-known actor who had also directed about a hundred films, including many of the early silent era's best Westerns—to California in 1914, the same year the Morrisons arrived. Like Francis, he took on the name of the automobile behemoth. Ford set about learning the business from the ground up—literally, as Francis delighted in commanding his younger sibling to perform stunts that left him on the floor, writhing in pain. John did a little acting, a little carpentry, a little editing, a little camera work—anything Francis demanded.

The brothers ended up at Universal, an up-and-coming outfit. In 1915 studio chief Carl Laemmle moved the company onto a 230-acre expanse that was the wonder of the industry. "I hope I didn't make a mistake coming out here," the mogul muttered as his employees trooped through the studio's decorative arch for the first time. Laemmle specialized in cheap movies that appealed to rural audiences. Westerns were Universal's strong suit, and Laemmle needed people who could churn out profitable pictures on time and on budget. John's cinematic bloodlines earned him a shot behind the camera, where he showed a knack for producing above-average pictures at a reasonable cost.

At Universal, Ford formed a partnership with Harry Carey, a former cowboy who became a star of Western films. The two dreamed up scenarios around the wood stove in Carey's kitchen, then filmed them in a rapid-fire, off-the-cuff style. Ford admired

Carey's spare performances. "He was a slow-moving actor when he was afoot," the director remembered. "You could read his mind, peer into his eyes, and see him think." Carey also entranced Marion Morrison, who consumed his films at Glendale's Palace Grand Theater, never dreaming that one day Ford would speak of him in the same way.

The director's silent-era Westerns possessed an honesty and a depth of character missing from the showy white hat/black hat melodramas that Carey's gun-slinging contemporary Tom Mix favored. *Straight Shooting* (1917), Ford's first feature-length production, found the director establishing motifs he would toy with for the rest of his life. In the film, Cheyenne Harry (Carey) takes the homesteaders' side in a cattle war even though he knows that the coming of civilization will render roughnecks like him obsolete—showing shades of John Wayne's Ethan Edwards in *The Searchers* (1956) or Tom Doniphon in *The Man Who Shot Liberty Valance* (1962).

Ford left Universal in 1920 for Fox. His output varied wildly over the next several years. It seemed he would direct anything, whether a Tom Mix

---

above TWO OF DUKE'S BIGGEST INFLUENCES, WESTERN STAR HARRY CAREY AND DIRECTOR JOHN FORD, SET UP A SCENE FOR *DESPERATE TRAILS*, 1921, WITH IRENE RICH. THE ACTRESS APPEARED ALONGSIDE WAYNE IN 1948'S *FORT APACHE*.

oater or an arty melodrama, so long as the bosses left him alone. *The Iron Horse*, his 1924 epic of the transcontinental railroad, confirmed his status as one of Hollywood's top directors while furthering his interest in American folklore, characters on the social fringes, and the conflict between civilization and the wilderness.

Actors showed up on time and followed Ford's instructions, or else. Intense though he was, Ford generally ran a quiet set. He scorned directors who strutted and shouted like martinets. Although a bully at times, he generally held his tongue,

chewing on his handkerchief while he waited for the perfect take. The crew of *Mother Machree* (1928) was therefore startled when he screamed at a laborer who failed to properly usher a gaggle of geese onto an Irish village set. "He was the most awkward prop man we ever had," Ford later said of his victim, Duke Morrison.

The criticism was unfair, and Ford knew it (although he certainly wasn't going to let the kid *know* that he knew it). This was how the director operated. He abused, belittled, and demeaned people to test their loyalty. Ford soon recognized

Duke's pristine work ethic and desire to learn. He saw something of himself in the young prop man, another former football player from the sticks desperate for the acceptance of an elder male.

Like gladiators after the games, the two men started swapping stories of their football glory days. Ford ordered Duke to assume the four-point stance of an interior lineman, then promptly knocked out his arms, causing his face to splat in the mud. As the director and crew doubled over with laughter, Duke suggested they try again. He snared Ford's legs and drove him to the ground. The set fell silent until Ford stood up, dusted himself off, and roared with laughter. Duke Morrison was in.

———————————— ☆ ————————————

"I like the way that kid walks," fellow Fox director Raoul Walsh told Ford. "He is a real pioneer type."

Ford agreed that Duke Morrison was a fine physical specimen. The directors scrutinized the odd jobber like an expensive cut of beef. He had impressive hands, wide shoulders, athletic grace, and a wholesome face that would look good under a cowboy hat. But could he act, Walsh asked? He can handle anything, Ford assured him.

Duke did whatever Ford asked of him. Round up some football players to serve as extras, carry

off that set, dive into that choppy sea, come drink with me—Duke was more than a man's man, he was Ford's man. Ford repaid Duke's obedience by arranging bit parts in minor films. Duke was something more than a prop man, but far less than an actor. That was about to change.

Walsh needed a leading man for an epic Western called *The Big Trail*. Tom Mix was shooting another film. So was Gary Cooper. Walsh felt immense pressure to find the right actor. Fox Studios had a lot riding on *The Big Trail*.

Studio head William Fox was in a good position to compete in the lucrative market that opened once Warner Bros.'s *Don Juan* (1926) and *The Jazz Singer* (1927) proved the viability of the Vitaphone sound-on-disc system. Fox's technicians had perfected Movietone, a process for recording sound directly onto film rather than onto discs, which could be damaged or lost. Fox poured millions into upgrading theaters, building sound stages, purchasing equipment, and hiring talent—hoping to monopolize the movie industry.

An antitrust suit was filed to block Fox's audacious plan and imperiled his empire. Fox needed a quick infusion of capital. Paramount's recent demonstration of widescreen films provided a possible solution to his woes. Fox believed that Grandeur Pictures, a 70 mm process that doubled

———————————— ☆ ————————————

opposite CINEMATOGRAPHER GEORGE SCHNEIDERMAN, CAMERA OPERATOR BURNETT GUFFEY, AND JOHN FORD SHOOT *THE IRON HORSE*, 1924, AN EPIC ABOUT THE TRANSCONTINENTAL RAILROAD. THE MOVIE SOLIDIFIED FORD'S STATUS AS ONE OF HOLLYWOOD'S TOP DIRECTORS.

the ordinary width of a movie screen, was as revolutionary as sound technology. He assigned Raoul Walsh to prove him right.

Walsh needed a leading man who not only looked good but sounded good. Many of Fox's silent-era stars had beauty but no voice. Recent imports from Broadway had voices suited more for drawing rooms than the frontier. Duke Morrison was ruggedly handsome and came cheap—no small consideration for a production that would require weeks of costly location shoots. He looked good in buckskin. But, Walsh wondered, could he talk?

Walsh arranged a screen test. Duke squirmed while another actor rattled off questions about leading a wagon train to Oregon. Duke had not seen the script and fumbled for answers. Eventually frustrated, he returned fire. "Where are you from?" he asked his inquisitor. "Why are you going West? Can you handle a rifle?"

Duke's gameness had impressed John Ford, and now it impressed Walsh. The director set up another test, this time with Duke clad in Western garb and a Stetson hat. Like many rookie actors, he overplayed his lines. His performance nevertheless satisfied Walsh. "He's the best we got," he concluded. "He's the only one we got." Duke Morrison, whose single screen credit was for an insignificant role in *Words and Music* (1929), would star in Fox Studio's biggest production to date.

There was one more detail to address. "Marion Morrison" was no name for a rugged Western hero. Walsh suggested "Anthony Wayne." Studio executives liked "Wayne"—it was strong, blunt, manly—but "Tony" felt too Italian and a little feminine. Someone tossed out "John" as a substitute. With that, Duke, who wasn't even in the room, both lost and gained an identity. The man upon the screen would be John Wayne.

Now John Wayne needed to learn how to act. Walsh sent Duke to see Fox's voice expert, a British Shakespearean actor named Lumsden Hare, who set about creating a Western version of Hamlet. Roll your r's, stretch your vowels, make your gestures grand, Lumsden insisted. Wayne quit after two weeks. "You're very wise, Mr. Wayne," Lumsden said. "You'll never be an actor."

Walsh dragged his cast through Arizona, Wyoming, Montana, and California to simulate the dangers pioneers faced as they rolled west. The director's Broadway ringers, however, did not seem to grasp the importance of the project. They drank prodigiously, complained about early-morning calls to the set, and whined about the heat. "They were a bunch of bums," Walsh fumed. "Full of booze, they over-acted ... John was the only one who knew his lines." At times it seemed Wayne was the only one

NOW KNOWN AS "JOHN WAYNE," DUKE FLASHES A YOUTHFUL SMILE DURING THE SHOOTING OF
THE BIG TRAIL, 1930. WAYNE'S RAW GOOD LOOKS HELPED HIM LAND THE PART, BUT EVEN EARLY IN HIS
CAREER HE USED HIS EYES AND UNDERSTATED GESTURES TO CONVEY MEANING IN THE STYLE OF
POPULAR WESTERN ACTOR HARRY CAREY.

FOX'S PUBLICITY CAMPAIGN FOR *THE BIG TRAIL*, 1930, EMPHASIZES THE PICTURE'S EPIC SCOPE AND GRAND SCALE. UNFORTUNATELY, IT WAS A BOX-OFFICE FAILURE THAT NEARLY DOOMED DUKE'S FRAGILE ACTING CAREER.

taking the shoot seriously. Unlike the veterans, he embraced Walsh's advice to stay on the proverbial wagon and resisted the urge to chase women.

Duke's performance as seasoned scout Breck Coleman stands out against a backdrop of hungover, hammy actors. Silent films required emotive faces and waving arms. Wayne sensed that talkies demanded the opposite. Remembering his conversations with John Ford, Wayne made Harry Carey his model. Plain talk. Simple clothes. Small gestures.

Act with your eyes. Don't act, react. His rawness showed whenever he slipped in and out of something approximating a southern accent or allowed Lumsden-esque flourishes to mar his restrained style. On the whole, however, he looked like a natural. He was relaxed yet taut, as comfortable leaning against a rifle as hurling himself into a foe.

Walsh shone the spotlight on Wayne in his first scene and never took it away. He appeared in the center of the screen, his immaculate, off-white

---

★

above WAYNE AS BRECK COLEMAN AND ZEKE (TULLY MARSHALL) GUARD THE WAGON TRAIN AGAINST AN ATTACK IN *THE BIG TRAIL*, 1930.

cigarettes to beat that face into a weatherworn visage conveying wisdom and experience.

Even so, it is possible to mark the moment in *The Big Trail* where "John Wayne" was born: Caught in a blizzard, some of the settlers urge retreat. Coleman will have none of it. In a rather windy speech, he connects their journey to a larger narrative of expansion and progress, linking the migrants to a spirit born in England and driving westward ever since Puritan days. "No great trail was ever blazed without hardship," he insists. Eventually, however, the savage wilderness will yield to civilization. Hard work, rugged individualism, law and order—these are the ideals that John Wayne would spend the next fifty years fighting for.

The Big Trail, though episodic and marred by uneven performances, was an entertaining film with some exciting set pieces. But it failed to recoup its $2-million production costs. William Fox's robust theater-buying campaign, which left him millions in debt, had the studio teetering on the brink of bankruptcy when the stock market crashed in October 1929. Fox resigned, leaving the studio in disarray just as its epic feature hit screens. Because only two theaters had converted to the 70 mm Grandeur process, most viewers watched the less-impressive 35 mm version. The sagging economy also discouraged ticket sales.

buckskins contrasting with everyone else's dark, tattered clothes, his light baritone rising above the other men's deep voices. He is the star, and the fate of the movie, to say nothing of the wagon train, rests on his broad shoulders. If anything he is too handsome. No one with teeth so bright and with skin so smooth could possibly be a grizzled scout. Wayne had not yet grown into his character. It would take years of sun, wind, rain, booze, and

Mixed reviews and poor box office meant disaster for Duke's budding career. Fox cast him in two films in 1931, the silly *Three Girls Lost* and the wretched *Girls Demand Excitement*, before terminating his contact.

Wayne was a free agent in the worst job market in American history. John Ford wasn't talking to him because the director took Wayne's friendship with Walsh as a personal betrayal. Westerns were on their way out now that *The Big Trail* convinced producers that urban markets rejected oaters. Josephine, after years of being a girlfriend, wanted to be a bride. But Duke was twenty-four years old and washed up with barely a penny to his name.

⭑

opposite THE BIG TRAIL DIRECTOR RAOUL WALSH USED WAYNE'S HEIGHT, HANDSOMENESS, AND CLOTHES TO EMPHASIZE HIS STATUS AS THE HERO. DUKE EXPLOITED THESE ATTRIBUTES WHEN HE LOCKED EYES WITH CO-STAR MARGUERITE CHURCHILL. *above* WITH MARGUERITE CHURCHILL, HELEN PARRISH, DAVID ROLLINS, AND WAYNE IN THE BIG TRAIL, 1930.

MAKING JOHN WAYNE

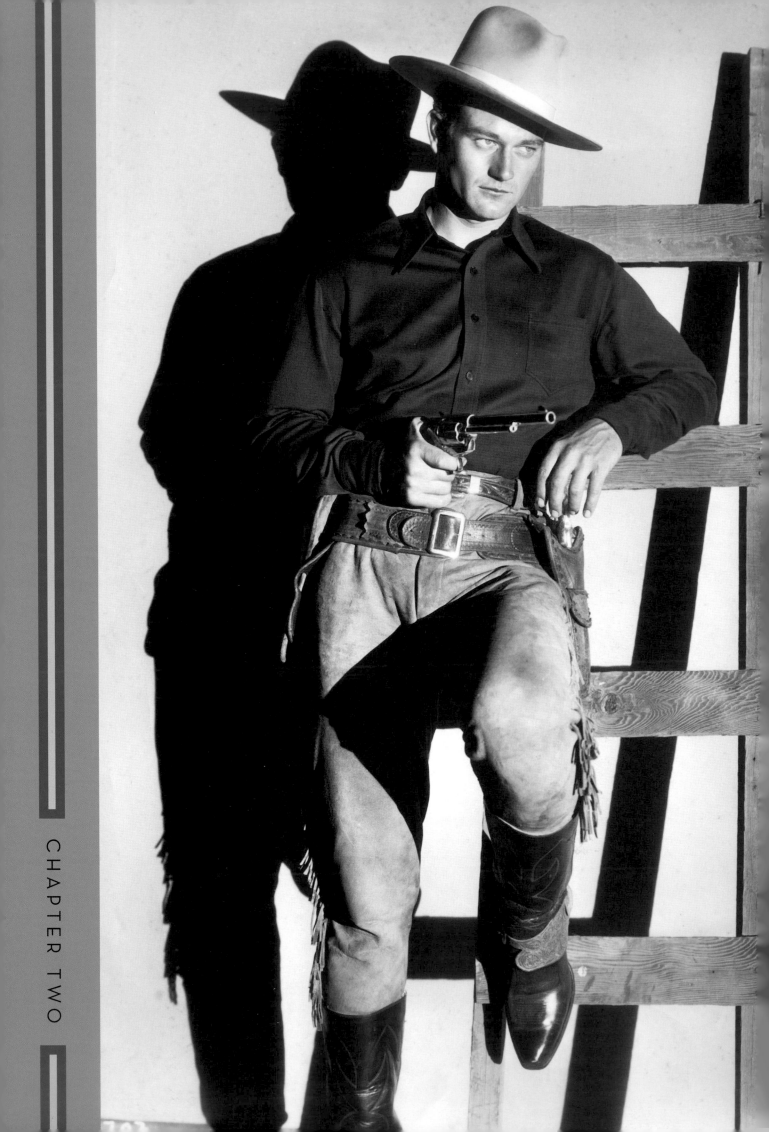

the WILDERNESS YEARS

"WHEN I STARTED I KNEW I WAS NO ACTOR AND I WENT TO WORK ON THE WAYNE THING ... IT WAS AS DELIBERATE A PROJECTION AS YOU'LL EVER SEE."

John Wayne wasn't the only one who needed a paycheck. Millions of Americans lost their jobs as the economy sank deeper into depression. In 1931, as wobbling banks called in farmers' loans and former businessmen sold apples in the street, lyricist E. Y. Harburg composed the quintessential anthem for a troubled era. "Say, don't you remember, I'm your pal," he wrote. "Brother, can you spare a dime?"

— ★ —

opposite WAYNE POSES AS JOHN TRENT FROM *THE TELEGRAPH TRAIL*, CIRCA 1933.

Hollywood, feeling the pinch, resorted to luring customers with gimmicks. Theater owners slashed ticket prices, sponsored giveaways, and ran double features to give patrons more bang for their entertainment buck. About four thousand movie houses closed anyway. Studios played it safe by churning out low-budget flicks that earned small but dependable profits from the second half of a bill. There was little prestige in making these films and little hope of using them to climb to stardom. But B-movies were still movies, and making movies meant work.

Wayne, who had some name recognition yet came cheaply, hooked on with Columbia, the most minor of the major studios. He fit well with studio chief Harry Cohn's penny-pinching philosophy. "Every Friday the front door opens and I spit a movie out into Gower Street," Cohn said. "I want one good picture a year ... That's my policy."

Columbia cast him as an army lieutenant in a trite quickie called *Men Are Like That* (1931), a film Duke hated almost as much as the critics. Worse, Cohn heard rumors from the set that his new talent was seducing leading lady Laura La Plante, whom Cohn had targeted for his own casting couch. Cohn didn't buy Duke's claim that he was guilty only of innocent flirtations. "When you're at this studio, you keep your pants buttoned!" he shouted.

A vengeful Cohn punished the actor's supposed transgression by using him as a corpse in *The Deceiver* (1931). Male lead Ian Keith had to leave town just after completing a scene where he gets murdered. For the next shot, Duke dressed in Keith's clothes and lay facedown on the floor with a prop knife sticking from his back. Other inconsequential roles followed before Cohn twisted the knife: In *Maker of Men* (1931) Wayne played a talentless college football player who sells out his team.

"I couldn't stand some of the old-time moguls," Duke remarked forty years later, "especially Harry Cohn." The two soon parted ways, leaving Duke to descend the Hollywood ladder by inking a contract with Mascot Pictures, a Poverty Row outfit that cranked out low-budget serials. Wayne's deal paid $100 a week, with a "week" entailing anywhere from seventy to one hundred hours on the set. Survival at Mascot was more about endurance than ability. Crew members held torches to light scenes shot before dawn and shone headlights to illuminate sets after dark. "We worked so hard ... we didn't have time to think," Duke remembered.

Wayne made three serials for Mascot: *Shadow of the Eagle* (1932), *The Hurricane Express* (1932), and *The Three Musketeers* (1932). None capitalized

on his talents. Serials delivered maximum thrills and a stirring cliffhanger in each fifteen-minute installment. There was no time for subtlety or character development. Scripts focused on moving the story forward and employed long speeches to remind viewers about earlier plot points.

Wayne's inexperience was obvious. He recited his lines, managing to sound both rushed and wooden, and moved like a hyperactive puppy that doesn't realize how big its feet are. His reaction shots were broad—his jaw gapes, his arms flail, his eyes bug out—and he looked clumsy when leap-frogging counters or diving through windows.

"They were rotten pictures," Duke said. Maybe so, but they also taught valuable lessons. As he had at Fox, Wayne haunted the set, hanging out with the crew and picking up tips wherever he could. He learned how to memorize lines and gained experience in action scenes. And, perhaps most importantly, he met Yakima Canutt.

★

---

above AFTER *THE BIG TRAIL* FLOPPED, WAYNE HONED HIS CRAFT IN FORGETTABLE SERIALS SUCH AS MASCOT'S *THE HURRICANE EXPRESS*, 1932, IN WHICH HE PLAYED A DARING PILOT WHO UNCOVERS THE HIDDEN IDENTITY OF "THE WRECKER" WHILE WOOING AN ENGINEER'S DAUGHTER (SHIRLEY GREY).

Legendary stuntman Enos Edward "Yakima" Canutt deserves much of the credit for "making" John Wayne. "I spent weeks studying the way Yakima Canutt walked and talked," Wayne told an interviewer. "I noticed that the angrier he got, the lower his voice, the slower his tempo. I try to say my lines low and strong and slow, the way Yak did."

Canutt left the rodeo circuit in the mid-1920s after deciding there was more money in falling off horses in front of the camera than in staying on them in front of an audience. Mascot signed him to coordinate stunt work and do some second-unit direction. He was a seasoned professional by the time Wayne arrived. Duke revered Canutt not just as a movie man, but as a man. He epitomized Duke's image of the cowboy. Canutt respected Wayne's determination and his refusal to put on airs around the crew. "Wayne [was] a regular kind of guy," he said. There was no greater compliment.

The two cemented their friendship one night in the wilderness north of Los Angeles. *Shadow of the Eagle* director Ford Beebe had shot until midnight and wanted everyone back at six the next morning. Most of the company spent the night outdoors rather than drive home. Wayne squatted before a campfire and produced a bottle of whiskey. Canutt knelt beside him. Duke handed the bottle to Yak, who took a slug and returned it. With that wordless exchange, the men began a collaboration that extended through *Stagecoach* (1939), the *Fighting Seabees* (1944), and *Rio Bravo* (1959).

Yak's friendship boosted Duke's credibility among the cowboys who served as extras. Under his tutelage Wayne learned how to ride, how to dress, how to draw a gun, how to talk, and how to walk. Duke's oft-imitated swagger was itself an imitation of Yak's swagger. As Wayne explained it, "I just imagine that I have a pea between the cheeks of my ass and I don't want to drop it."

Wayne's rise as an action star rested upon Yak's talents. The two spent hours choreographing barroom brawls and mastering realistic ways to throw stage punches. Duke did many of his own stunts, but Yak handled the most spectacular ones. When John Wayne leaped onto a speeding train, clung to a stagecoach, or jumped from one horse to another, it was really Yak risking his neck. At times Yak had to chase himself, tearing across screen on his horse for one take, then changing into Wayne's clothes and doing it again, making sure to ride cleaner when the star was supposed to be on camera.

So, in a way, John Wayne and Yakima Canutt were one and the same.

——————————— ★ ———————————

Wayne was not yet seen as a Western hero. His contract with Mascot allowed him to work with other studios, and he played a variety of small roles in several Paramount and Warner Bros. pictures between 1932 and 1933. Most were forgettable, although he did land an interesting, if most un-John Wayne–like, role as femme fatale Barbara Stanwyck's hapless boy toy in the excellent *Baby Face* (1933). Warner was interested in Duke primarily because he resembled silent-era Western actor Ken Maynard. They dressed up Wayne in Maynard's costumes, shot some new scenes with him, and mixed the footage into dubbed versions of the original films to create something approximating a seamless blend. These inexpensive, recycled productions did brisk business in rural

———————————————— ★ ————————————————

opposite DUKE IDOLIZED FORMER RODEO RIDER YAKIMA CANUTT (LEFT), WHO TAUGHT HIM HOW TO WALK, TALK, RIDE, AND FIGHT IN FRONT OF A CAMERA. THEIR PARTNERSHIP ENDURED FOR DECADES. HERE THEY SHARE A SCENE WITH LANE CHANDLER (CENTER) IN *SAGEBRUSH TRAIL*, 1933.

DUKE MARRIES HIS LONGTIME COLLEGE SWEETHEART JOSEPHINE SAENZ, JUNE 28, 1933.

B-markets. Duke earned $1,500 per picture, enough to put food on the table during the Depression's worst months.

It was also enough to convince Wayne to finally tie the knot with Josephine. Their June 1933 wedding was one of the high points on that year's society scene, not because of Duke, an obscure actor with few prospects, but rather because of Josie's family. "Consul Saenz's Daughter Bride of Marion Morrison," read a *Los Angeles Times* headline.

Poverty Row beckoned as soon as Duke said "I do." With no major studios calling, Wayne signed a deal with Monogram. "My main duty was to ride, fight, keep my hat on, and at the end of shooting still have enough strength to kiss the girl and ride off on my horse, or kiss my horse and ride off on the girl," he joked. Duke was being modest, if only a bit. Monogram made cheap films targeting rural southern and western audiences. Their generic titles reflect their predictability—*Riders of Destiny* (1933), *Sagebrush Trail* (1933), *West of the Divide* (1934). They stand almost as parodies of legendary producer Jesse Lasky's "Famous Players in Famous Plays" slogan—rather Formulaic Players in Formulaic Plays.

Audiences expected a Monogram picture to give them fifty-five minutes of action, fancy riding, and one-dimensional characters. Each new Wayne

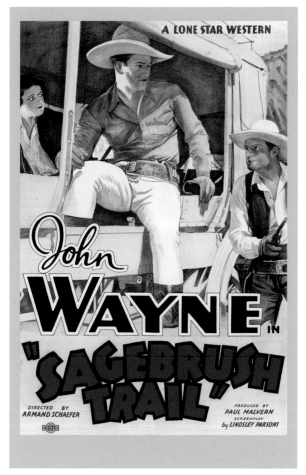

film was a rewrite of the last one. A stranger, played by Wayne, rides into a town where a land baron, a cattle thief, or an evil businessman threatens good-hearted commoners. Wayne's character mobilizes the oppressed and defeats the bad man, restoring order and facilitating the onward march of civilization. And along the way he gets the girl.

The ethos of these pictures fit the heady first days of the New Deal. Roosevelt's inauguration promised a renewed assault on the Depression and, after Herbert Hoover's disastrous term, raised hopes

---

★

---

above BY 1933 JOHN WAYNE WAS A BIG NAME IN SMALL PICTURES. FORMULAIC OATERS SUCH AS *SAGEBRUSH TRAIL* PUT FOOD ON THE TABLE AND GAVE DUKE AN OPPORTUNITY TO PERFECT HIS ACTING SKILLS.

for the kind of effective leadership that Wayne's characters provided. Monogram's Westerns, like many contemporary Americans, held out-of-control capitalists responsible for social ills. "The people" themselves were good, needing only a strong hand to rally them to fight for civilization over economic savagery. Some of these pictures, including *Riders of Destiny* and *The Star Packer* (1934) reinforced faith in Roosevelt by depicting the people's savior as a special agent sent from Washington, DC.

JOHN WAYNE — 'RANDY RIDES ALONE' WITH GEORGE *Gabby* HAYES
A LONE STAR WESTERN RE-RELEASE

Duke's sixteen Monogram Westerns, routine as they were, featured touches that elevated them above standard B-movie fare. Cameraman Archie Stout, who later won an Oscar for *The Quiet Man*, did exceptional work on these films. Along with director Robert Bradbury, he created a compelling vision of the West that shunned the geological splendor that John Ford brought to many of his pictures. Monogram's West was a scrubby panorama of sagebrush and rocky hills. It had no soaring peaks and no majestic valleys. It was a workingman's West, a hard place where men test themselves just to scrape out a living.

The Monogram pictures also showcased Yak Canutt's spectacular stuntwork. His elaborate mounts and convincing brawls brighten the moody landscape without turning the films into flashy fabrications. Canutt made endangering his life look effortless. Perhaps his greatest moment came in 1934's *Randy Rides Alone*. Yak, doubling for Wayne, barrels his horse across a bridge with the bad guys in hot pursuit. In one unbroken motion he hurls

---

★

---

opposite WAYNE IN *THE STAR PACKER*, 1934. *above* MOVIE POSTER FEATURING WAYNE AND YAK CANUTT BRAWLING IN *RANDY RIDES ALONE*, 1934. THE TWO FRIENDS SPENT COUNTLESS HOURS REHEARSING WAYS TO MAKE STAGED FIGHTS LOOK REAL.

himself off the horse and over a high guardrail before executing a perfect dive into a river running some twenty feet below.

For Duke, his confidence grew as he incorporated lessons from Harry Carey, John Ford, and Yak Canutt, as well as from ace dialogue coach Paul Fix. He was becoming "John Wayne." He gained control over his body, working out his nervous tics and establishing a realistic cowboy image. "I figured I needed a gimmick, so I dreamed up the drawl, the squint, and a way of moving meant to suggest that I wasn't looking for trouble but would just as soon throw a bottle at your head as not." His rolled trousers and low-slung holster emphasized his pigeon-toed stride and swaying hips. He mastered the art of standing as if there was nowhere in the world he'd rather be. His vocal delivery slowed and acquired gravitas. Audiences now listened when he spoke.

John Wayne was a cowboy star by the mid-1930s. Although unknown to most big-city movie fans, he had a definite screen image and a loyal following on the oater circuit. But appreciative audiences in the rural South, West, and Southwest were not enough to interest major studios, which regarded Monogram's films as distasteful and disreputable. Duke had to keep scuffling, grinding out a career one picture at a time.

His situation improved in 1935 when a former American Tobacco Company executive named Herbert Yates merged several Poverty Row companies to form Republic Productions. Yates did not know much about making movies, but he excelled at making money. Republic offered Wayne the opportunity to work with better actors and bigger budgets. As an added bonus, his two-year, $48,000 contract obligated him to make only eight Westerns, a luxurious schedule compared to his hectic Mascot and Monogram days.

Westward Ho (1935), Duke's first Republic film, showed off every penny of its $34,000 budget. It marked the first time since *The Big Trail* that Wayne operated in a majestic-looking West. Unlike Monogram's scrubby wasteland, *Westward Ho* featured wide valleys and snowcapped mountains. Wayne, too, seems more impressive. He moves with grace and ease, and his vocal cadence is rounding into shape. His advancing age served him well; the callow youth of *The Big Trail* had turned into a rugged man. Close-ups of his face and eyes reveal depths missing five years earlier. The only real misfire comes when Duke has to strum a guitar and lip-sync a tune. The dubbed voice could not have sounded any less like his own. Wayne had nothing against Gene Autry and Roy Rogers, the two other horses in Republic's talent

stable, but the singing cowboy business wasn't for him. He wanted something that felt real.

Westward Ho brought new scenery but the same old plot. In the role of John Wyatt, Duke again played a mysterious stranger who brings order to a community under attack from lawless elements. As often happened in these films, there is a case of mistaken identity, this time of Wyatt's long-lost brother, Jim. Duke gets off on the wrong foot with the female lead (Sheila Mannors), only to win her over at the end. Civilization's conquest of savagery is again the underlying theme.

Westward Ho was dedicated to the men who domesticated the frontier, and Wayne's character was

⎯⎯⎯⎯⎯⎯⎯⎯⎯⎯⎯⎯⎯ ★ ⎯⎯⎯⎯⎯⎯⎯⎯⎯⎯⎯⎯⎯

above WAYNE SERENADES SHEILA MANNORS IN *WESTWARD HO*, 1935, HIS FIRST FILM FOR REPUBLIC STUDIOS, AND ONE OF SEVERAL WHERE HE HAD TO PLAY A SINGING COWBOY, A ROLE HE HATED.

clearly part of that process. The same is true of his and Republic's *Winds of the Wasteland* (1936), a tribute to those who linked the nation through the telegraph, as well as *The New Frontier* (1935), *The Lawless Range* (1935), and *The Oregon Trail* (1936). Devious outlaws and unscrupulous businessmen impede progress. In defeating them, Wayne renders his original character obsolete because there is no need for vigilantes in the new West. Unlike some of his later efforts, he does so without reservation or remorse. He seems

JOHN WAYNE TREASURES

content to marry the girl, build a house, and settle down to a quiet life in a bustling community.

Duke, having become one of Republic's leading box-office draws, took another shot at the big time by jumping to Universal to star in a series of action films. "I was ambitious and wanted to vary my pictures," he explained. Universal was looking for a sweet spot between A- and B-movies, films that could reach urban audiences without costing too much. Duke played in six forgettable, if well-regarded, pictures in a variety of roles. He played a Coast Guard commander, an owner of a trucking company, a hockey player, a boxer, a pearl diver, a cameraman. None of them catapulted him to real stardom.

He limped back to Republic when his Universal contract expired in 1937. Herbert Yates did not exactly welcome him back with open arms. Duke accepted a one-third cut in salary to star in eight "Three Mesquiteers" films that placed him alongside Ray Corrigan and Max Terhune as a team of gunmen who ride into towns, defeat a bad man, and establish law and order. Wayne's character got to kiss the girl in the last scene. Terhune carried a ventriloquist's dummy named Elmer. Duke never wanted to talk much about those movies.

In keeping with the Western's New Deal allegiances, the Three Mesquiteers series dropped occasional references to Washington as an ally in the war for civilization. "With the Mesquiteers behind us, we're bound to get a new deal," a settler enthuses in *Santa Fe Stampede* (1938). That same film features a U.S. Marshal—a federal agent—who helps the Mesquiteers outwit a band of corrupt local politicians.

Offscreen, Wayne rarely thought about politics. He considered himself a Roosevelt Democrat, a liberal who believed the federal government could help the common man. At the same time he was developing a stage persona who believed exactly the opposite. Over time he absorbed the ethos of the cowboys who populated his pictures. Time and again he played a virile male, an individualist, a man who laughed in the face of power. "John Wayne" needed no government assistance, felt no desire for outside interference. "The West," Duke sighed, "the very words go straight to that place of the heart where Americans feel the spirit of pride in their Western heritage—the triumph of personal courage over any obstacle whether nature or man." Heroic pioneers carried freedom and democracy to the unenlightened frontier. Individuals, not governments, tamed the wilderness.

———————— ☆ ————————

Although John Wayne was standing tall, Duke needed someone to lean on. Studying himself in

———————— ☆ ————————

opposite WAYNE SCUFFLES WITH FRANK RICE AND HANK HARVEY IN *THE OREGON TRAIL*, 1936, ONE OF DOZENS OF B-WESTERNS THAT CAST DUKE AS A WHITE-HATTED HERO DETERMINED TO PROTECT CIVILIZATION FROM BLACK-HATTED THUGS.

the mirror, he saw a man fast approaching middle age. He had made over sixty films and received few accolades. There seemed little chance of breaking through to stardom.

His marriage to Josephine was on the rocks. The couple had four children between 1934 and 1940 but found little else to hold them together. Josie inhabited a high-class world of cocktails and tuxedoes. She found her husband's career both trivial and demeaning. Wayne, never comfortable with women, drifted ever farther away. Day after punishing day on the set left him with little time or energy to be a father. His family woes compounded when his father, Clyde Morrison, died in 1937. Duke lost a flawed but essential male presence.

He sought comfort in the company of men, especially with his mentor John Ford. Wayne never knew why Ford refused to speak to him for three years, and he never knew why the prickly director then invited him onto his boat, the *Araner*, for drinks one day in 1934.

Duke climbed aboard the yacht apprehensively. It was like stepping into another world, one of polished teakwood opulence. The *Araner* had two fireplaces, two bathrooms, red carpet, a four-poster, and a dressing room for Ford's wife, Mary. In the central salon was a large poker table, where Ford could usually be found holding court.

Wayne approached. Ford was telling a story, surrounded by a group of friends. Without looking up he said, "Hi, Duke, sit down," and continued his tale, as if Wayne's arrival was the most natural of occurrences. Later, when the others were getting into the shore boat, Ford asked, "Duke, could you stay for dinner?" And that was it. The deepest friendship in John Wayne's life was back on course.

"To this goddamn day I don't know why he didn't speak to me for [those] years," Duke later told Ford's grandson Dan. Ford was not a man for explanations, and John Wayne was not one who needed them.

Once they reconciled, the two were inseparable. Wayne became part of a hard-drinking band that included Henry Fonda, screenwriter Dudley Nichols, and Ward Bond, a blowhard actor who had played football with Duke at USC. Ford was the ringmaster. Wayne, who viewed him more as a father figure than a friend, affectionately called him "Coach" no matter how much abuse the director heaped upon him. Leaving Josie on the mainland to take care of the kids, Duke and the rest of the gang boozed it up for weeks at a time on the *Araner* before going their separate ways. Everyone returned to the major studios except Duke, who tramped back to Poverty Row to don another hat, save another town, and share screen time with a puppet.

---

opposite WAYNE SPENT MUCH OF THE 1930S GRINDING THROUGH TWELVE-HOUR DAYS ON SET IN MODESTLY BUDGETED FEATURES. HE BECAME A TALENTED RIDER EVEN THOUGH HE NEVER REALLY LIKED HORSES.

CHAPTER THREE

STAGECOACH: *the* REINVENTION *of the* WESTERN

"DON'T EVEN FOR A MINUTE MAKE THE MISTAKE OF LOOKING DOWN YOUR NOSE AT WESTERNS ... THE OLD WEST WILL NEVER DIE."

In 1938, four years after they had healed their rift, Ford again summoned Duke to the *Araner*. Wayne expected the usual crew of friends, perhaps a writer like Dudley Nichols or Liam O'Flaherty or an actor like Henry Fonda or Johnny Weissmuller, and certainly the ever-present loudmouth Ward Bond. But Ford was alone with the crew. He handed Duke a script that Nichols had recently written. It was based on a short story by Ernest Haycox that had been published in *Collier's* magazine. The tale, titled "Stage to Lordsburg," detailed a desperate stagecoach ride through Native American country and a shoot-out between the hero and his enemies. Ford had bought the movie rights for

───────────── ✦ ─────────────

opposite WAYNE IN *STAGECOACH*, 1939—WHERE HE, ALONG WITH FORD, WOULD ELEVATE WESTERNS TO A NEW LEVEL FOR THE AMERICAN PUBLIC. *STAGECOACH* ALLOWED DUKE TO ESCAPE LIFE ON POVERTY ROW.

$7,500. Nichols's script had stayed basically true to the story, though the screenwriter had cut a few of the characters and added a couple of others.

No one knew better than Duke that Westerns were out of fashion. Ford had cut his teeth on the genre but had not made a Western in over a decade. Since the coming of sound, he had made a film about the Great War, a few comedies with Will Rogers and Stepin Fetchit, and an assortment of historical biopics, adventure movies, and socially earnest productions. None of them had anything to do with the Wild West.

So Wayne was surprised by the script. Set in the West—much of it on a stagecoach—it had a prostitute with a heart of gold; a greedy, thieving banker; a drunken, socially conscious doctor; a comedic stagecoach driver; a couple of stiff-backed southern aristocrats; and several other stock Western characters. And most of all, it had a Western hero, the Ringo Kid, a wrongly convicted, escaped prisoner who was a good man to have around when it came to gun play.

What Duke read sounded familiar. Its setting, plot, and characters were similar to the B-Westerns he had been making throughout the decade. Of course it was better written and structured, and in the hands of John Ford it would undoubtedly transcend the genre, but all the same it cried out

for a tall, silent, white-hatted Western hero, a good bad man just like John Wayne. Was Ford thinking of casting him, Duke wondered? Or was he cruelly toying with him?

"You are acquainted with some of the new young actors," Ford said. "I was wondering if you knew of one that could play the Ringo Kid?"

Wayne suggested Lloyd Nolan. Nolan had played the heavy in Paramount's *The Texas Rangers*, one of the best A-Westerns of the mid-1930s. His performance had drawn good reviews. But he was not right for the Ringo Kid. That role required youth, strength, and gun-handling skills, and something more—it demanded innocence and even gentleness. Not the role for a heavy.

"Nolan?" Ford reacted, dismissing the suggestion. "Jesus Christ, I just wish to hell I could find some young actor in this town who can ride a horse and act. Duke, you must know someone. But then you've been out at Republic. You're not likely to see a hell of a lot of talent out there."

For the next few days while they sailed off the southern coast of California, Ford baited Duke, criticizing his pictures and his career. Wayne took it, as he always did. Finally, as the yacht was docking at San Pedro, Ford said, "Duke, I want to tell you something. I have made up my mind. I want you to play the Ringo Kid."

WAYNE IN *STAGECOACH*, 1939. DIRECTOR JOHN FORD HANDPICKED WAYNE FOR THE ROLE. JUST AS FORD HAD GIVEN DUKE HIS FIRST JOB IN THE INDUSTRY, NOW HE MADE HIM A STAR.

Duke felt as if he had been "hit in the belly with a baseball bat." Ford was offering him a ticket out of B-Western purgatory. At that moment, a glimmer of the actor John Wayne would become momentarily flashed before him.

———————— ★ ————————

Ford's timing was perfect. Across America in the mid-1930s a new sensibility was taking shape. It could be heard on the radio, read in popular novels, and watched on the silver screen. It was an ode to America, harkening to the notion of American exceptionalism. During a decade that saw Nazis threaten Europe, Italian fascists menace Africa, Japanese imperialists bully Asia, and Soviet communists brutalize their own people, many Americans believed that democracy itself was under attack, and as a result they clung tighter and looked deeper at their political and social institutions.

In Hollywood musicals and along Tin Pan Alley, the early 1930s had been a time of glamour and sophistication. Except for E. Y. Harburg's hit "Brother, Can You spare a Dime?" the Great Depression was something to escape from rather than to refer to. From "It Had to Be You" to "Thanks for the Memories," songwriters such as George and Ira Gershwin and Cole Porter embraced Americans' love of falling in, being in, and falling

out of love. In the movie palaces of the country, Fred Astaire gave form to the hit-makers' lyrics and music, gliding across the surface of America's dreams with the grace and sophistication of his top hat, white tie, and tails.

John Wayne fit uncomfortably into the Hollywood of glamour and glitz. He lacked the grace of Astaire and looked more comfortable in jeans and a cowboy hat than a tuxedo. This sophisticated sensibility in Hollywood was one of the reasons Duke could only find work at B-studios like Republic. And he knew it. There were times in the first half of the decade when he considered looking for a new line of work. Yet acting was the only career he had, and any work was hard to find during the Great Depression.

But Hollywood and Duke's luck were about to change. A new feeling emerged in the music and theaters of America. The most striking but by no means the only example of this shift in popular tastes was Irving Berlin's "God Bless America," a bold hymn to the songwriter's adopted land. Its sense of impending threat, feeling for the American landscape, and bold declaration of a "land that I love" signaled the new direction of American popular culture. By the last years of the 1930s, Americans couldn't get enough of America.

This was the period when the phrases "the

American way of life" and "the American Dream" came into usage, the time when writers penned best-selling books about the national character. Folklorists studied the American folk at the same time as Woody Guthrie gave a voice to those same people. "This Land Is Your Land" beautifully expressed the democratic nature of America at the same time as it celebrated the country's mesmerizing beauty. Perhaps only an Okie like Guthrie—and a few others—could see the splendor in America's "diamond deserts" and "dust clouds rolling." In most cases, the land that Guthrie extolled was the American West, the landscape of the B-Westerns of the period.

above DIRECTOR JOHN FORD ON THE SET OF *STAGECOACH* IN MONUMENT VALLEY, 1939. WHO FIRST THOUGHT OF SHOOTING FILMS IN MONUMENT VALLEY IS AN OPEN DEBATE, BUT FORD MADE THE PLACE FAMOUS.

The West, John Wayne believed, held a special place for Americans. John Ford also appreciated the West of deserts and mountains, and with the script he was now calling *Stagecoach*, he sought to return to the country he loved at the very time when the national mood pined for that return.

But the road from script to movie was rocky. Ford needed financing. At the time his production company was associated with David O. Selznick, who hated the idea of an ensemble Western with no big star. He judged *Stagecoach* "just another Western," the sort of film that was suitable for a nobody like John Wayne but not a premier director like John Ford. As film historian Scott Eyman noted, "Selznick was not completely off track; within the context of the period, 'Western' meant little more than a B-movie, and 'classic Western' was an oxymoron."

Ford and his partner at Pioneer Pictures, Merian Cooper, explained the importance and potential of *Stagecoach* as a new breed, a "classic Western." Slowly, Selznick began to come around. Perhaps with a few big name stars—maybe Gary Cooper and Marlene Dietrich—the script's love interest could be built up enough to give the film box-office punch, he thought.

But Ford and Cooper had already promised the lead roles to Wayne and Claire Trevor, and besides, the use of iconic stars would unbalance the ensemble nature of the cast. The two passed on Selznick's suggestion and continued their search for an ideal producer—a man with money, class, and enough faith in Ford to keep his hands out of the scripting, casting, and shooting process. They found their man at institutionally laissez-faire United Artists. Walter Wanger was the product of an Ivy League education and understood the idea of reinventing the Western genre. Even more important, his ego was not such that he needed to micromanage every decision.

This is not to say that he was happy with all of Ford's ideas. Like Selznick, Wanger had no faith in John Wayne. As far as he was concerned, the name John Wayne cried out "B-Western." Why not use like Joel McCrea? Why not anybody with a better reputation than Wayne? But Ford refused to budge. Wayne was right for the role, he insisted. He would not compromise on either his word to Duke or his vision of the film. Knowing better than push too hard, Wanger acquiesced.

———————————— ✦ ————————————

Ford quickly filled out the rest of the cast. He had already selected Claire Trevor for the crucial role of Dallas, a prostitute who had been run out of Tonto by the ladies of the Law and Order League, a gaggle of blue-nosed hypocrites. Trevor had been

———————————— ✦ ————————————

opposite WAYNE WITH CLAIRE TREVOR, THE PROSTITUTE WITH A HEART OF GOLD, IN *STAGECOACH*, 1939. THE PAIN ON TREVOR'S AND WAYNE'S FACES MARKED THEM AS OUTCASTS, REFUGEES FROM THE MARGINS OF AMERICAN LIFE.

STAGECOACH POSTER

Movie poster for *Stagecoach* featuring Claire Trevor, Andy Devine, John Wayne, Donald Meek, and John Carradine, 1939.

CIGARETTE CARD

Wayne featured as the Western hero on a movie star cigarette card, 1930s.

opposite WAYNE IN COSTUME FOR *STAGECOACH* SET, 1939. HE HAD YET TO LOSE HIS BOYISH LOOKS.

e Frontier

THE RINGO KID

BANKER NAMED GATESWOOD
JOINED PASSENGERS MYSTERIOUS-
LY AT EDGE OF TOWN, CARRYING

...t

Nine oddly
Mexico. Ea
Then stran

As co
together. C
the surface
the Americ

(Due
recon

nominated for a best supporting actress for her role of a sick prostitute in *Dead End*, and she brought a particular sad-eyed, pained poignancy to a part. She looked like a woman who had been mistreated by life, ready to wince when anyone raised a hand near her. Cast opposite Wayne's Ringo Kid, the contrast between experience and innocence would be powerful. They were both victims of society, only Ringo was too inexperienced to realize it.

The other roles went to seasoned character actors. Andy Devine (Buck) played the stagecoach-driving Falstaff; John Carradine (Hatfield) the Southern gentleman down on his luck; Thomas Mitchell (Dr. Josiah Boone) the drunken physician who had seen too much suffering for one life; Donald Meek (Samuel Peacock) the mild-mannered liquor drummer; George Bancroft (Sheriff Curly Wilcox) the efficient yet sympathetic lawman; Berton Churchill (Henry Gatewood) the pompous, crooked banker; and Louise Platt (Lucy Mallory) the Southern female ideal painfully unable to overcome her class instincts. It was an ensemble cast, each character and pair of characters playing off against the others to explore such themes as social prejudice, sacrifice, redemption, western democracy, individual reinvention, and the American character.

Ford believed his reinvention of the Western genre had to appear fresh and visionary on the screen. He got wind of a place called Monument Valley. Years later, Ford told his grandson that George O'Brien, an actor who had often appeared in the director's films, told him about place. But Ford was never a reliable source on the facts on anyone's life, especially his own. More likely Ford heard about Monument Valley from Harry Goulding, a man who defies easy description. He was tall, and looked even taller because of his wiry frame and cowboy boots, which he wore on virtually every occasion. In the early 1920s he first set his eyes on Monument Valley—and it was love at first sight.

Monument Valley looked as if it had been built as a playground for dinosaurs—immense, otherworldly, and sublime. Over the eons, wind and rain had carved its Chelly sandstone mesas into outcrops of towers, many a thousand or more feet high. Scott Eyman thought the red-striped buttes resembled "fists punching through the earth's crust." There is a pitiless, almost violent aspect to the place. But there is also a deep, ever-shifting beauty. It is kaleidoscopic, changing colors with the time of the day and the effects of dust and rain.

Not long after Goulding first saw Monument Valley, he moved there with Leone, whom he called Mike, a strikingly beautiful woman he had just married. It might have seemed like they were moving to another planet. Monument Valley lay on a 30,000-

acre strip of northeast Arizona and southeast Utah, about 175 miles from Flagstaff. It was one of the most inaccessible places in America. In the 1930s, no place in the country was as far away from a railroad, and probably no site had fewer roads.

Monument Valley belonged to the Navajos, and Harry set up a trading post, and raised some sheep on the side. But in the 1930s, during the Depression and a series of droughts, life got hard. Tucked away from the rest of the country, the people in the valley seemed invisible.

It was then that Harry Goulding decided to take the initiative. Hearing that some director was going to shoot a new Western movie, he drove to Hollywood and made a pitch for Monument Valley. Carrying an album of haunting Josef Muench

---

above THE BEAUTIFUL MONUMENT VALLEY, 1939—THE SET FOR WAYNE'S FIRST SUCCESSFUL EPIC WESTERN, *STAGECOACH*. HARRY GOULDING INTRODUCED FORD TO BEAUTIES OF THE OTHERWORLDLY SPOT.

7

JOHN WAYNE AS THE RINGO KID, *STAGECOACH*, 1939. THOUGH OTHER CHARACTERS HAD MORE LINES,
HE IS THE MORAL CENTER OF THE FILM.

photographs of the land, Goulding found his way to John Ford's office and refused to leave until someone gave him an audience. A location manager finally looked at the photographs, then immediately called Ford. The director was stunned. He later called Monument Valley the "most complete, beautiful, and peaceful place on earth." Not only did he find a place to shoot *Stagecoach*; he discovered his spiritual home, a place he would return to again and again to make Westerns.

Ford and photographer Bert Glennon spent only seven of the forty-seven production days in Monument Valley, but the scenes and landscapes they shot would give *Stagecoach* its otherworldly look.

At its basic level *Stagecoach* is concerned with the fragility of life. The film is populated by suffering souls. What caused Doc Boone to become a drunk, or Dallas a whore, or Hatfield a gambler, or Peacock a frightened rabbit of a man? What trapped Lucy

above GEORGE BANCROFT, JOHN WAYNE, AND LOUISE PLATT ON THE INFAMOUS STAGECOACH, *STAGECOACH*, 1939. ONLY DANGER CAN STRIP AWAY CLASS DIVISIONS.

into her psychological cage, or twisted Gatewood into a platitude-spouting crook? The enormity of Monument Valley, the magnificent scope of some of Ford's shots, underscores the precarious state of human life and relationships. The stagecoach wending across hostile Native American country is isolated by the land. Nowhere in America could the director have found a landscape to match the film's interior drama. Monument Valley became iconic the moment it filled a frame.

And Monument Valley set the stage for John Wayne's emergence as an icon. To be clear, *Stagecoach* is an ensemble production, along the lines of *Grand Hotel* (1932), but from the beginning, Ford intended to make John Wayne a star. In Haycox's short story, Malpais Bill (the Ringo Kid in the film) is on the stage to Lordsburg at the beginning of the journey, but Ford and Nichols changed it in the script. In the film, Ringo does not make his first appearance until almost the nineteenth minute. Before then, he is only mentioned and discussed, creating a mood of anticipation.

Then a rifle shot and he appears on-screen, a saddle under his left arm, a Model '92 Winchester in his right hand, framed against the stark beauty of Monument Valley. Not known for camera flourishes and tricks, Ford broke all his rules introducing Wayne. In a dolly shot, moving so quickly from a long shot to a close-up that the camera momentarily loses focus, the face of John Wayne, caked with dust and streaked with sweat, fills the screen. It is a breathtaking scene, "one of the most stunning entrances in all of cinema," judged Western film authority Edward Buscombe.

"Hold it," Ringo commands.

"Hey look, it's Ringo," Buck cries out in delight.

"Yea. Hello, Kid," says Curly in a flat, cautious voice, his shotgun pointed at Ringo.

"Hiya, Curly," Ringo guardedly replies. Then with a quick, open smile he adds, "Hello Buck, how's the folks?"

With one scene John Wayne established a character he would play for the rest of his life.

His outfit—placker-front, button-down wool shirt, army-style braces, neckerchief, dusty working-man's jeans worn outside of the boots, not an article of cowboy-slick on his body—mirrored his character. His accent is American, an amalgam of the South, Midwest, and West, with a trademark halting delivery. There is not the hint of anything eastern or sophisticated about him. He is a man made for the harsh western land.

Ford's star treatment of John Wayne did not end with Ringo's first scene. Ringo is the moral center of *Stagecoach*. He sees the world innocently, judging the other passengers on their merits as humans, not their family background or social position. Wayne registers his opinions not with words but looks. Throughout the film Ford's camera focused on Duke's face for reaction shots. "People think I'm an action actor," Wayne was fond of saying. "It's not true. I'm a reaction actor."

Ford struggled to wring the performance out of Wayne. The director was famous for tormenting actors. He seemed to sense who could take it and not push back, and went after them with a vengeance. Whether it was Victor McLaglen in *The Informer* (1935), Harry Carey, Jr. in *Three Godfathers* (1948), or Ward Bond whenever he was around, Ford usually singled out some actor in each film for nonstop abuse.

---

opposite WAYNE ON SET OF *STAGECOACH* WITH DIRECTOR JOHN FORD AND THE CREW. FORD MADE SURE DUKE GOT THE ROLE. THEN HE TORTURED HIM THROUGHOUT THE SHOOT.

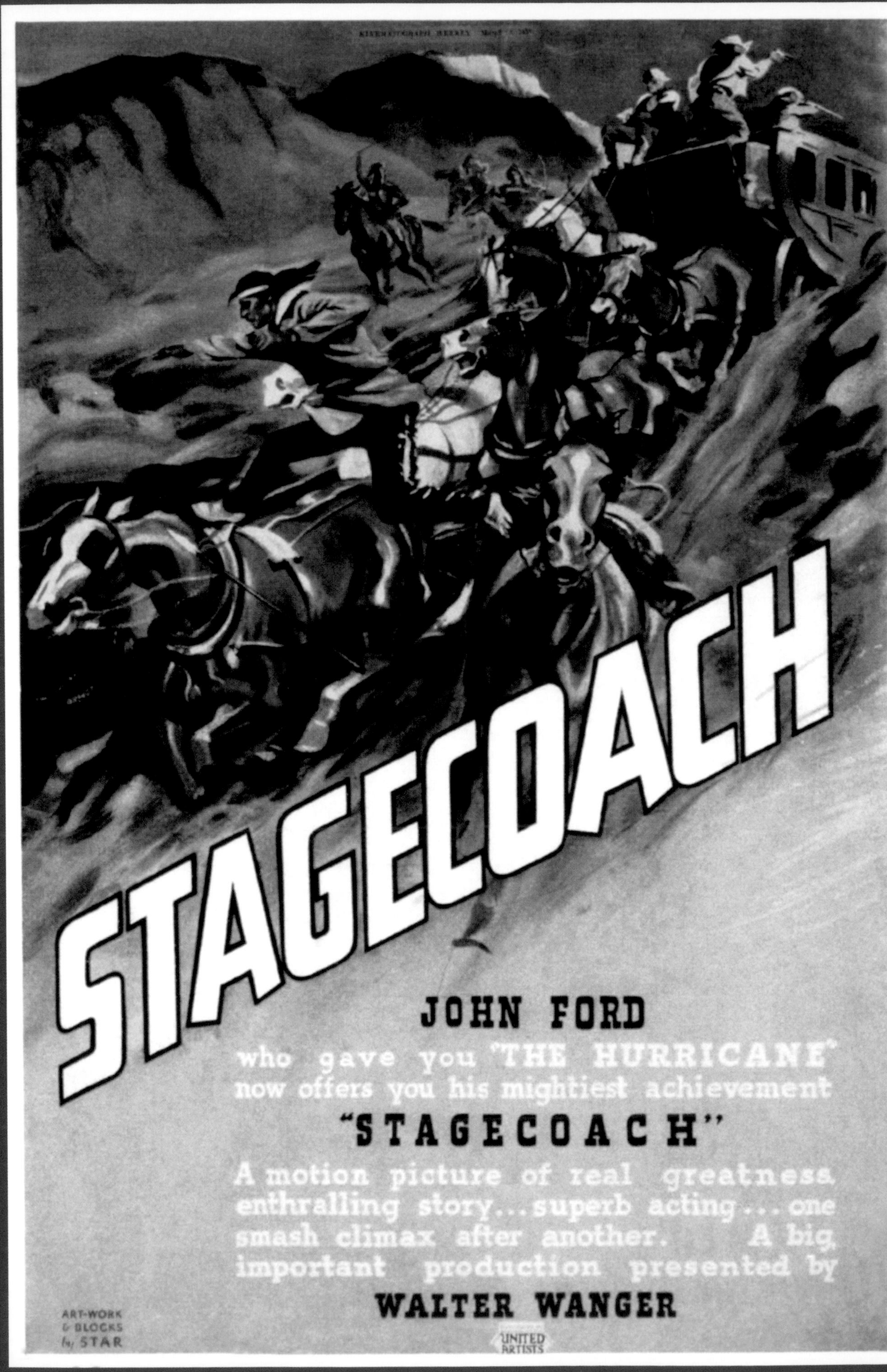
STAGECOACH
JOHN FORD
who gave you "THE HURRICANE"
now offers you his mightiest achievement
"STAGECOACH"
A motion picture of real greatness, enthralling story... superb acting... one smash climax after another. A big, important production presented by
WALTER WANGER
ART-WORK & BLOCKS by STAR
UNITED ARTISTS

On the *Stagecoach* set, it was Wayne. It started with Duke's screen test. Displeased with the actor's attempt to express emotions with his mouth, Ford stopped the camera. "Ford took Duke by the chin and shook him," Claire Trevor recalled. "Why are you moving your mouth so much? Don't you know that you don't act with your mouth in pictures? You act with your eyes."

Ford was right, even if his method was harsh. And it continued throughout the filming of *Stagecoach*. He called Wayne a "big oaf," a "dumb bastard," and much worse. "It was tough for Duke to take, but he took it," said Trevor.

It was a small price to pay for stardom. Wayne's performance, shot against Monument Valley and accompanied by a score that featured American folk classics, was a tour de force. When *Stagecoach* was released in 1939, reviewers gushed over everything about the film. After watching the film at Radio City Music Hall, *New York Times* reviewer Frank S. Nugent wrote, "John Ford has swept aside ten years of artifice and talkie compromise and has made a motion picture that sings a song of camera. It moves, and how beautifully it moves, across the plains of Arizona, skirting the sky-reaching mesas of Monument Valley, beneath the piled-up cloud banks which every photographer dreams about … Here, in a sentence, is a movie of the grand old school, a genuine rib-thumping and beautiful sight to see."

To a degree unmatched in the history of Hollywood, Wayne, Ford, and Monument Valley seemed so perfectly suited that they virtually merged into a single entity. Years later, a biographer asked Wayne what separated him from such others B-Western idols as Bob Steele, Tim McCoy, Tex Ritter, Roy Rogers, and Gene Autry.

Duke thought for a moment, took a drag off a cigarette, and smiled: "John Ford."

Had he thought a second moment he might have added: "Monument Valley."

When *Stagecoach* was released in 1939, it rode into cinematic history. From the first it was recognized as a classic, the birth of the adult Western.

For Hollywood, 1939 was an *annus mirabilis*. It saw the release of *Mr. Smith Goes to Washington, Destry Rides Again, The Wizard of Oz, Young Mr. Lincoln*, and, most famously, *Gone With the Wind*. It was a year that celebrated America on the silver screen, one that witnessed the Hollywood studio system demonstrate the full range of its genius.

In retrospect it could be argued that *Stagecoach* was at the center of the brilliance. Writer Buzz Bissinger accurately observed that the film "created three icons": John Wayne, John Ford, and Monument Valley. And it recreated the Western movie.

---

opposite STAGECOACH, 1939, DELIVERED JOHN WAYNE OUT OF THE B-WESTERN DESERT AND MADE HIM A STAR. EVEN THE STYLIZED POSTER ART SUGGESTS THE HEART-PUMPING DRAMA OF THE PERILOUS STAGECOACH RIDE THROUGH HOSTILE TERRITORY.

CHAPTER FOUR

COMING
of the WAR

"I'M LUCKY TO HAVE SURVIVED THE DOZENS OF
B-PICTURES I MADE. THEY KILLED OFF MANY
FINE ACTORS."

John Ford was convinced that war was coming to the United States. He couldn't relax, couldn't get the idea out of his head. Duke, Ward Bond, and the other passengers on the *Araner*'s Christmas 1939 cruise just wanted to play cards and get drunk. They didn't want to talk about the so-called *sitzkrieg* that settled over Europe after Britain and France declared war on Germany in September, and they didn't want to talk about the ongoing war between China and Japan. But Ford, a lieutenant commander in the Naval Reserves, kept prattling on about the Japanese menace to America.

Ford spent hours at the rail, scanning the shoreline and studying other ships in the Gulf of California for evidence of Japanese mischief. An innocent-looking

---

opposite JOHN WAYNE IN *DARK COMMAND*, 1940, ONE OF THE HIGHER-BUDGET
FILMS HE APPEARED IN AFTER HITTING IT BIG WITH *STAGECOACH*.

(too innocent-looking?) Japanese shrimp-boat fleet caught his eye. The sailors seemed too well dressed, too tall, too good-looking, too well groomed, to be ordinary fishermen. Ford thought they looked like Samurai warriors—definitely military. Wayne and his companions egged on Ford, who was convinced that he had stumbled on some kind of intelligence-gathering operation aimed at establishing a toehold in the Western hemisphere.

Ford's paranoia was one expression of Hollywood's growing antifascism. Warner Bros. released *Confessions of a Nazi Spy*, the first major feature to overtly attack Hitler, several months before the *Araner* left port. MGM's *The Mortal Storm* (1940), Charlie Chaplin's *The Great Dictator* (1940), and Twentieth Century-Fox's *Man Hunt* (1941) highlighted the crowded field of anti-Nazi films that were being produced.

Hollywood also released a spate of flag-waving movies that encouraged nationalism and emphasized the wonders of democracy. A slew of historical films including *Abe Lincoln in Illinois* (1940), *Northwest Passage* (1940), and *Young Tom Edison* (1940) celebrated American decency, ruggedness, and ingenuity as traits that could thrive only in a democracy. World War I dramas such as *The Fighting 69th* (1940) and *Sgt. York* (1941) delivered heaping doses of patriotism while stressing the need for a diverse nation to unite in the face of totalitarian threats.

Hollywood socializing took on a distinctly political sheen. Cocktail parties buzzed with news of the Spanish Republicans. Mass meetings—something decidedly foreign to the apolitical movie community of a few years earlier—heralded the arrival of the Hollywood Anti-Nazi League. Bundles for Britain's shop on Sunset Boulevard raised money to aid refugees. James Cagney, Melvyn Douglas, Edward G. Robinson, and other film folk issued a Declaration of Democratic Independence urging President Roosevelt to sever trade ties with Germany.

None of these movies, activists, or groups called on the United States to enter the war. Indeed, they accepted FDR's argument that the best way to aid in the war effort was to support Great Britain's fight against Germany. Some powerful Hollywood voices hesitated to say even that much. Industry elders remembered the abuse they took after World War I, when disillusioned Americans argued that a string of hysterically anti-German films had contributed to the United States' decision to enter the fight.

The war was pulling Wayne's employers, friends, and colleagues in strange new directions, and he was caught in the middle. John Ford pressured him to get involved in the war-preparedness

cause. Duke wanted nothing to do with it. He "never talked politics … couldn't even spell politics," Henry Fonda claimed. Duke maintained friendships with both liberals and conservatives and viewed the war as a distant thing. "John Wayne," however, made a living speaking other peoples' words and was therefore immersed in politics no matter how much Duke wanted to stay out.

Above all else Wayne concentrated on advancing his career. Having had a taste of A-movies after a decade of Bs, he refused to slip back down the ladder. "I did a lot of thinking about the quickie Westerns I'd been making," he said, "and began to realize that they were a one-way street. You could last in them only as long as your brawn held up, but they certainly wouldn't take you anyplace except

above WAYNE STOLE THE SHOW IN JOHN FORD'S *STAGECOACH.* REPUBLIC STUDIOS, HOWEVER, SHOVED HIM BACK INTO FORMULA WESTERNS SUCH AS *WYOMING OUTLAW*, 1939, WHERE HE AGAIN DUKED IT OUT WITH GOOD FRIEND YAKIMA CANUTT.

62

into the next one." Duke thought he was going places when he made *The Big Trail*. Now, after *Stagecoach*, he had a second chance to consolidate his fragile grip on stardom.

───────── ★ ─────────

After *Stagecoach*, Duke tried to escape the typecasting that confined him throughout the 1930s. While horses and cowboy clothes had made him a minor star, he never really liked horses and preferred suits and ties over boots and flannels. During the next few years he ping-ponged from studio to studio, alternating between roles that stretched him and roles that required him only to play John Wayne.

Republic welcomed its new star back to the fold with open arms that immediately tossed him into four more Three Mesquiteers films. *The Night Riders*, *Three Texas Steers*, *Wyoming Outlaws*, and *New Frontier*, all from 1939, rode across B-movie screens while *Stagecoach* played at A-theaters. Republic, eager to capitalize on Wayne's growing box-office appeal, expanded his part with each film until he stood as the first among equals.

More important roles in unimportant pictures. "Duke was never very good at hiding his feelings, and you could tell he wasn't happy about returning to those awful six-day Westerns," his longtime secretary said. He gave it his all, tried to make the

best possible movie out of what he was given, but oaters could not satisfy him anymore. Conferences with studio head Herbert Yates won him a better deal. Republic agreed to treat Wayne as an A-list star, pumping up his films' budgets and giving him leading roles while granting him the freedom to shoot pictures with other studios.

Bigger budgets did not always translate into better movies. *A Man Betrayed* (1941), *Lady from Louisiana* (1941), and *Lady for A Night* (1942) were, to be polite, routine pictures. Two of Wayne's Republic projects from this period did, however, aspire to and occasionally realize something better than average: *Dark Command* (1940) and *Three Faces West* (1940).

Republic budgeted *Dark Command* at a hefty $750,000, more than it had ever spent on a film. It boosted the picture's prestige by borrowing Walter Pidgeon from MGM and reuniting Wayne with *The Big Trail* director Raoul Walsh. Yak Canutt contributed some fine stunts. Republic also brought in Claire Trevor in an attempt to recapture the *Stagecoach* magic. Together, they managed to pull another rabbit from their collective hat. *Dark Command* was no masterpiece, but it was a solid piece of screen entertainment. Duke again meshed nicely with Trevor and exhibited a comedic touch that surprised many reviewers. Wayne "impressively

───────── ★ ─────────

opposite IN *DARK COMMAND* REPUBLIC STUDIOS TRIED TO RECAPTURE THE MAGIC OF *STAGECOACH* BY REUNITING WAYNE WITH CLAIRE TREVOR. THE FILM WAS SHOT AT PLACERTIA RANCH IN NEWHALL, CALIFORNIA.

Duke still wanted to stretch himself with roles that got him out of the saddle and, he assumed, into more theaters. *Three Faces West*, his next project, offered a middle ground by transporting his established cowboy character into the present-day Dust Bowl. Written mostly by Samuel Ornitz, who later got caught up in Hollywood's anticommunist blacklist, it was an earnest—probably too earnest—attempt to blend entertainment with education, using theater as a tool for commenting on current events.

Ornitz penned a complicated, twisting screenplay about an Austrian doctor, Dr. Karl Braun (Charles Coburn), and his daughter, Leni (Sigrid Gurie), seeking refuge from the Nazis in the rural American community of Asheville Forks. The farmers are at first suspicious of the foreigners in their midst. John Phillips (Wayne) leads the forces of tolerance, encouraging his fellow farmers to accept the new arrivals while urging the Brauns to drop their Old World allegiances and become true Americans. "You stopped being a refugee when you came through Ellis Island," he tells them.

The picture veers in a different direction when the townspeople, with Phillips again in the lead, abandon their windswept farms for the lush valleys of Oregon. Raoul Walsh should have directed *Three Faces West* instead of *Dark Command*, as the film's

carries off one of his best roles," *Variety* observed. He benefited from a good script that adapted the story of pre–Civil War Bleeding Kansas and Missouri border raider William Quantrill into a bang-up horse opera with a compelling love triangle. *Dark Command* returned big dividends on Republic's investment, grossing more money than any other picture the studio released that year. It solidified Wayne's status as a top Western attraction and again demonstrated that the genre could appeal to A-movie audiences.

second half is essentially an updating of *The Big Trail*, with Wayne leading a line of cars rather than wagons over the mountains and into the promised land to the west. Present-day Americans rekindle the pioneer spirit as they brave snowy passes and scorching deserts.

Wayne is offscreen when *Three Faces West* lurches into overt anti-Nazism. In an unnecessary plot twist, Leni's former fiancé, Eric (Roland Varno), meets her in San Francisco. He has betrayed his friends, joined the Nazi Party, and perhaps played some role in brokering the recent Nazi-Soviet Pact. Now he wants the Brauns to become his partners in abetting Germany's drive to acquire new territories. Horrified, the Brauns reject his proposal. The good doctor offers a warning on his way out. "You look so perfectly healthy," he tells Eric, "and yet you have become infected with a disease more malignant than cancer, a disease that will be fatal to you and millions of your countrymen."

Ornitz's attempt to blend epic drama with politics left audiences and reviewers unsatisfied. Wayne received good notices, a hopeful sign as he tried to branch out. But reviewers saw *Three Faces West* as a hackneyed attempt to cash in on *The Grapes of Wrath* (1940) and thought its anti-Nazi flourishes preachy and amateurish.

Such criticism captured the paradox of Wayne's

career with Republic. He was an accomplished leading man struggling to overcome the studio's shortcomings. His work outside of Republic brought a different problem: Major studios offered more resources and better talent but refused to let him carry a movie.

——————————— ★ ———————————

"*Long Voyage Home* was right after *Stagecoach*," Duke remembered in 1972, "but I was still doing six-day Westerns. I'd finished one at twelve o'clock at night and the next morning I had to start a picture where I was a Swedish sailor … I wanna tell you, that was quite a switch from the night before, knocking people around and jumping on a horse." In fact, Wayne was indulging in a false memory (he completed *Three Faces West* the night before, not some B-movie oater), but his point was valid. John Ford's *The Long Voyage Home*, an adaptation of four Eugene O'Neill one-act plays, was unlike anything he had ever tackled.

Ford was a cinematic polyglot who confounded his followers with genre switches and unusual casting choices. His three previous films had offered folksy perspectives on Okies (*The Grapes of Wrath*), a chesty interpretation of the American Revolution (*Drums Along the Mohawk*), and an introspective take on the Great Emancipator (*Young Mr. Lincoln*).

———————————— ★ ————————————

opposite MOVIE POSTER FOR *THREE FACES WEST*, FEATURING WAYNE AND SIGRID GURIE, 1940. SCRIPTED BY ANTI-FASCIST SCREENWRITER SAMUEL ORNITZ, THE FILM HAD WAYNE BATTLING BOTH THE ELEMENTS AND THE NAZIS.

COMING OF THE WAR

Now, as he had in *The Informer*, his 1935 master-piece about the Irish Revolution, he consciously set out to create an art film. His work with legendary cinematographer Gregg Toland produced a story of angst-ridden sailors haunted by their pasts and despairing for their future, told through an nihil-istic fog of claustrophobic shots, slashing beams of light, and ominous shadows.

It was, in other words, exactly the kind of movie that John Wayne had no business being in. And, in a sense, he wasn't. John Wayne, the swaggering gunslinger who kissed a hundred girls and saved a hundred towns, is nowhere to be seen. Instead there is Ole Olsen, a grinning naïf who loves his compa-triots and wants more than anything to return to his native Sweden.

Why Ford gave him the role is a bit of a mystery. Wayne feared he was not up to the part. Good reviews on a prestige picture could confirm his acting chops. Negative reviews might get him kicked back to Poverty Row. Duke worried that audiences would laugh at his accent or at the very idea of him playing a good-natured innocent. Ford reacted in his typical, mean spirited way when Wayne asked for a dialogue coach. "Well, Jesus, all right, if you want to be a goddamn actor," he replied.

Wayne understood the importance of *Long Voyage Home*, and so did Ford. Its world of hard-drinking men adrift at sea, of guilt and anger, of male companionship, resonated in the director's soul. Ford treated the shoot with deadly seriousness. He kept a silent set, except for the soft accordion music wafting over the proceedings, each piece selected to reinforce the mood of the current scene. Ford nervously rubbed his face as his actors rehearsed and peered through Toland's viewfinder to make sure every shot was perfect. No motion or inflection escaped his notice; he needed every actor to precisely capture his vision of a scene.

Wayne's job for the first three-quarters of the film was to blend in with the crowd. He is not the star of *Long Voyage Home*, but rather a key element of an outstanding ensemble cast that included Barry Fitzgerald, Thomas Mitchell, and

opposite DIRECTOR JOHN FORD (CENTER) WITH THE CAST AND CREW OF *THE LONG VOYAGE HOME*, 1940. WAYNE, STANDING BEHIND FORD, WORRIED THAT THE ROLE OF SWEDISH SAILOR OLE OLSEN WAS BEYOND HIS ACTING ABILITY. *above* WAYNE WITH CARMEN MORALES IN AN UNCHARACTERISTICALLY UPBEAT PROMOTIONAL PHOTO FOR *LONG VOYAGE HOME*.

John Qualen. Still, it is clear that there is something special about this boy. His bright white shirt and megawatt smile separate him visually from his dour shipmates. Ole stretches dreamily in the sun, immune from the others' pain. He thrives on memories of home while his crewmates have given up all hope of ever finding one. "Best thing to do with memories is to forget 'em," argues Paddy (played by Bob Perry, whose pipe and round glasses give him a close resemblance to Ford).

Wayne's moment arrives in the film's final act. The *Glencairn* has put ashore and its crew is determined to get Ole safely aboard his ship to Stockholm. They've been here before, so close to saving Ole from a grim life at sea, only to have something go wrong. For several terrifying minutes it seems history will repeat itself as Ole gets snared by a prostitute who drugs his ginger beer. With his mates off carousing in the back, Ole gets dragged to a ship with an unscrupulous captain needing another deckhand.

This sequence marked Duke's only extended time on-screen. It required him to be passionate yet vulnerable, determined to get home yet foolish enough to tell a dockside hooker about the cash sewn into his coat. His accent held true throughout, and screenwriter Dudley Nichols compressed maximum emotion into minimal dialogue. When

asked how he teased out such a marvelous performance, Ford said, "Count the times Wayne talks ... That's the answer. Don't let him talk unless you have something that needs to be said."

As ardent antifascists, Ford and Nichols could not help but refer to contemporary troubles. Unlike Ornitz in *Three Faces West*, they show a deft touch, attacking the Nazis in a way that adds to the film's overall mood. Fascism lurks as an underlying menace, an additional piece of context darkening an already pitch-black atmosphere. Even Driscoll's (Thomas Mitchell) stagey speech, a clear reference to external events, feels right in this climate. "Blackout, blackout," he grumbles. "Everyone stumbling around in the dark. Is there to be no more light in the world? Is there no place in this dark land where a man who's drunk can find a decent bit of fun?"

Bosley Crowther of the *New York Times* called *The Long Voyage Home* "a modern Odyssey—a stark and tough-fibered motion picture which tells with lean economy the never-ending story of man's wanderings over the waters of the world in search of peace for his soul." Crowther said nothing about it being a crowd pleaser, and it wasn't. *Long Voyage Home* was too bleak to be endearing and too morally ambiguous to win mass audiences. It did, on the other hand, garner six Oscar nominations while

proving that Wayne was capable of more than rid-ing a horse and clobbering outlaws.

Duke's other pictures for the majors were less artistic but more profitable. Universal's *Seven Sinners* (1940) paired him with Marlene Dietrich, who was enjoying a career revival on the heels of her comic Western *Destry Rides Again*. *Seven Sinners* had her in familiar territory, playing an exotic café singer named Bijou ("just Bijou") who tosses *bon mots* to crowds of adoring men. "I'm a baaad influence," she moans as sailors driven insane by her mere presence start a battle royale for her attention. Wayne, as Lieutenant Daniel Brent, wins her love, only to lose it when Bijou gives him up to save his career with the navy. As was so often the case in Wayne's films, duty trumped lust.

---

above THE SMOLDERING CHEMISTRY BETWEEN MARLENE DIETRICH AND JOHN WAYNE IN *SEVEN SINNERS* GREW IN PART FROM THEIR TORRID OFFSCREEN AFFAIR. BY NOW DUKE'S MARRIAGE TO JOSIE WAS LITTLE MORE THAN A SHAM.

blooded American male would have done under the circumstances," Duke later explained.

By then Duke's marriage to Josie existed largely on paper. Wayne harbored painful memories of his parents' divorce and hoped to spare his children from repeating his experience. Josie and Duke, however, had nothing in common. Exhausted from his days on the set, he evinced little interest in black-tie formals. Josie, cultured socialite that she was, thought John Ford, Ward Bond, and Duke's other movie buddies a pack of boorish louts. Distant though they were, Duke insisted that Josie put him at the center of his world. He desperately wanted her to respect his career and his friends. She never could fill this need.

Duke's extramarital relationship with Dietrich was an open secret. Wayne described her as "the most intriguing woman I've ever known." They began appearing together in public, and he installed the actress in a hotel near the set of his next film, *Shepherd of the Hills*, a big-budget, Technicolor adaptation of novelist Harold Bell Wright's tale of a rough-hewn Ozark mountain clan. Like *Grapes of Wrath*, *Sgt. York*, *Jesse James* (1940), and *Tobacco Road* (1941), it's an entertaining piece of hillbilly chic that explores a backwater region where country folk make blood oaths, bootleg moonshine, and perform elaborate rituals before entering haunted grounds.

Seven Sinners was a Dietrich vehicle. Duke, although receiving second billing, disappears for most of the film's first half. Dietrich also took charge of their offscreen relationship. According to Hollywood myth, Dietrich wooed Duke by inviting him to her dressing room and inquiring, "I wonder what time it is." Lifting her skirt to reveal a watch fastened to her garter, she cooed, "It's very early, darling. We have plenty of time." One wishes the story were true, and perhaps it is. What is certain is that Duke proved receptive to Dietrich's repeated advances. He did "what any other red-

Duke jumped at the chance to work alongside his idol, Harry Carey, who received third billing but was the real heart of the film. Their scenes crackle with intensity and carry a quiet, understated tension. Wayne showed off a range of emotions in his role as Young Matt, a rugged moonshiner whose love for a good girl conflicts with his promise to kill his father (Carey), who left his mother in her time of need. At different moments he is tough, driven, tender, awkward, innocent, funny, and obsessed. By now he could impart meaning with a roll of the head, a tuck of the chin, a raise of the eyebrows, or a flick of the eyes.

Released in summer 1941, *Shepherd of the Hills* offered no insights into democracy or the menace of fascism. Wayne too remained mute as the world went up in flames. Other Hollywood films and figures took more overt positions. For example, *Man Hunt*, which appeared a month earlier, concerned a British sportsman hoping to bag Adolf Hitler. Darryl F. Zanuck and other studio heads were forging ties to the United States military. At Zanuck's

---

opposite MARLENE DIETRICH VAMPS IT UP WHILE WAYNE ASSUMES A SECONDARY ROLE IN *SEVEN SINNERS*.
above WORKING WITH HARRY CAREY IN *SHEPHERD OF THE HILLS*, 1941, WAS ONE OF THE GREAT THRILLS OF DUKE'S LIFE.

cue, two thousand Twentieth Century-Fox employees signed a statement pledging President Roosevelt "their loyalty and service, unconditionally and without reserve." The navy called up John Ford that fall. He ran his own organization, the Naval Field Photographic Unit, and worked under General William "Wild Bill" Donovan of the Office of Strategic Services. Congressional isolationists, fearing that the studios, most of them run by Jews of Eastern European descent were turning "17,000 theaters into 17,000 daily and nightly mass meetings for war," convened hearings in September to investigate whether Hollywood had become part of a warmongering propaganda machine.

Wayne was sorry to see Ford go, but these developments meant little to him. *Shepherd of the Hills* was a box-office hit, and he was a man with ambition. In interviews Wayne expressed a desire to play heavies, to take on character roles, to be an Actor. Harry Carey's wife, Olive, tried to smack some sense into him. "You are a big, dumb son of a bitch," she snapped. "The people have told you how they like you. They're your audience. You give them what they want, not what you want." Duke would follow her advice for the rest of his career. On the eve of Pearl Harbor he was a star. By war's end he was well on his way to becoming an icon.

⭐

opposite WAYNE AS YOUNG MATT IN *SHEPHERD OF THE HILLS*, 1941. *above* BETTY FIELD AND WAYNE IN *SHEPHERD OF THE HILLS*. THE FILM, A FAVORITE WITH AUDIENCES, ALLOWED DUKE TO PLAY A NUANCED CHARACTER WHILE GIVING HIM AN OPPORTUNITY TO WORK ALONGSIDE HIS HERO, SILENT WESTERN STAR HARRY CAREY.

the WAR *that* MADE JOHN WAYNE

"SURE I WAVE THE AMERICAN FLAG. DO YOU KNOW A BETTER ONE?"

By 1965, the scene had become so familiar that it bordered on cliché. John Wayne was fighting World War II yet again, this time as Captain Rockwell Torrey in Otto Preminger's *In Harm's Way*. Japanese planes had just attacked Pearl Harbor, and Rock Torrey had sailed his command out to look for the enemy fleet. After an engagement with a Japanese sub, his ship hit and his arm broken, he encounters his second in command, Commander Paul Eddington (Kirk Douglas). Eddington, his face streaked with grease and sweat, exclaims, "Oh, Rock of Ages. We got ourselves another war. A gut-bustin', mother-lovin' Navy war!"

---

opposite JOHN WAYNE IN *FLYING TIGERS*, 1942. AS AMERICA WENT TO WAR, JOHN WAYNE BECAME ONE OF THE TOP LEADING MEN IN HOLLYWOOD.

"It does seem to shape up that way, Commander Eddington," Torrey replies.

On December 7, 1941, when the Japanese actually did bomb Pearl Harbor, John Wayne was not so decisive. At the time, his career was on a sharp assent. In 1941 he made five films—*A Man Betrayed, Lady from Louisiana, The Shepherd of the Hills, Lady for a Night,* and *Reap the Wild Wind,* although the last two would not be released until early 1942. Three of the films were standard Republic fare, but the other two were major productions. *The Shepherd of the Hills,* directed by the talented Henry Hathaway, gave Duke a chance to stretch his acting range. And *Reap the Wild Wind,* directed by the legendary Cecil B. DeMille, was a big-screen spectacular.

As a leading man John Wayne was not yet in the same company as Gary Cooper, Clark Gable, Errol Flynn, Henry Fonda, or Tyrone Power, but he was definitely inching closer. In terms of his career, the war could not have come at a worse time. He was thirty-four years old, and though his marriage to Josie was in trouble, he was still technically married and a father of four. Always a realist, he must have sensed that as a romantic leading man, he did not have many years left to make his mark. The decision that he faced after Pearl Harbor—indeed, that millions of men across the nation faced—was what part he would play in the real war. Should he enlist? Or were there other options?

Thousands of men from the motion picture industry pondered the same choices. Thousands enlisted without hesitation. John Ford, the closest man John Wayne had to a father figure, had already been activated from the Naval Reserves. Henry Fonda also enlisted. Though thirty-seven, married, and a father of three, Fonda quietly drove to the naval headquarters in Los Angeles. And so did many other leading men. Jimmy Stewart and Gene Autry enlisted in the U.S. Army Air Corps; Clark Gable and William Holden in the U.S. Army; Robert Montgomery in the U.S. Navy; and Tyrone Power in the U.S. Marines. Along with millions of men and women in America, they felt it was their duty to serve their country in uniform.

At the beginning of the war Wayne's marital status and dependencies placed him beyond the reach of the draft. In addition, a series of physical problems plagued him. The shoulder he had hurt at USC had never fully healed, and he suffered from chronic inner-ear infections, a condition worsened by working underwater in *Reap the Wild Wind.* Furthermore, he worked in an industry important to the war effort and rich in draft exemptions. Only weeks after Pearl Harbor, President Franklin Roosevelt proclaimed, "The American

opposite JOHN WAYNE IN *REAP THE WILD WIND,* 1942. DIRECTED BY CECIL B. DEMILLE, THE FILM GAVE WAYNE STAR BILLING.

motion picture is one of the most effective media in informing and entertaining our citizens. The motion picture [industry] must remain free in so far as national security will permit." In February 1942, General Lewis B. Hershey, director of Selective Service, underscored the importance of the industry by instructing officials in California to grant deferments to men active in the movie-making business.

Throughout the war, deferments kept Wayne out of harm's way. At the start of the war he was classified 3-A, "deferred for dependency reasons." Later, when the government regularly began to call up men with dependents, Wayne was reclassified 2-A, "deferred in support of national health, safety or interest," the standard Hollywood deferment. Just before D-Day, as the demand for troops in both Europe and the Pacific became critical, he was

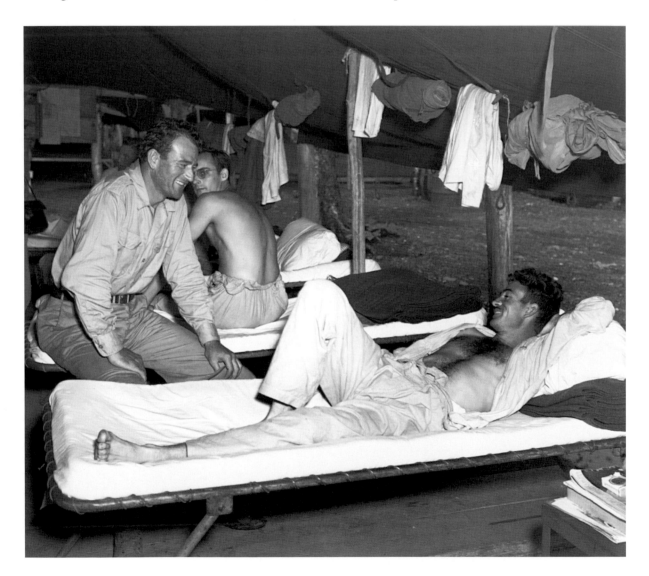

reclassified once again, this time to 1-A, "available for military service." But a lightning deferment claim changed his classification to 2-A. By the end of the war, he had once again been reclassified, this time to the safe 4-A deferment on the basis of his age.

In short, Wayne spent most of World War II in Hollywood making movies. Throughout the early years of the conflict he considered enlisting, even going so far as trying to get into Ford's Field Photographic Unit. And he traveled overseas on USO tours to the South Pacific and Australia. Along with other USO performers, he entertained troops from Brisbane, Australia, to New Britain and New Guinea. Often wearing a Colt .45 on his right hip, he signed autographs and talked with the troops, sitting up late into the night drinking their high voltage "jungle juice" and swapping stories of the battlefront and the home front.

In later years, after Wayne became an outspoken Republican conservative and a defender of the United States' involvement in Vietnam, liberal politicians would take potshots at his war record, pointing out what they believed was the hypocrisy of his position. He wanted American boys to fight in Vietnam when he did not serve in World War II, they argued. To the end of his life, he remained sensitive to the charges, perhaps wishing that,

like Ford, Fonda, Gable, and 16.3 million other Americans, he had served in uniform. But that does not diminish the service he did perform. Like the steel workers, coal miners, and farmers who worked on the home front, John Wayne and Hollywood contributed to the war effort.

Hollywood, and popular culture more generally, was critical during the war years. For Americans on the home front, World War II was to a great degree a war of imagination. It took no leap of imagination to comprehend the nature of the war for people living in the Soviet Union, Poland, Germany, France, Italy, China, Korea, and the other war zones, regions where bombs destroyed building and bridges, and in many cases soldiers raped and killed civilians. For them the war was a matter of survival.

In the United States, however, war felt far removed from everyday life—a distant echo from a far-off shore. While many Americans raged with the desire for revenge after Pearl Harbor, many were uncertain about the causes and goal of the conflict.

The role of popular culture was to give a face to the enemy and inform the public about the deeper nature of the conflict. The music industry, for example, immediately responded to the outbreak of war, turning out such jingoistic songs

---

opposite DUKE TALKS WITH SOLDIERS IN NEW GUINEA, 1944. FOR THE REST IF HIS LIFE HE REGRETTED HIS DECISION NOT TO SERVE IN THE WAR.

as "You're a Sap, Mr. Jap" and "The Japs Don't Have a Chinaman's Chance." Eventually the music industry released songs that touched the hearts of Americans. "I'll Be Seeing You" and especially "White Christmas" stirred Americans' imaginations and hearts, promising a better world when the enemy was vanquished.

Similarly, the comic book industry pitched in and did its part to help win the war. Not only did Captain America, Batman and Robin, Wonder Woman, and other favorites of the comics enlist, but the entire industry worked overtime turning out product with war themes. Story lines encouraged cooperation with the country's allies and stressed the need to ration goods at home.

Hollywood, however, occupied the central position in American popular culture, and the government turned to the industry's moguls to spread its war message. Under the Office of War Information (OWI), the Roosevelt administration created the Bureau of Motion Pictures (BMP), which reviewed scripts, advised producers, and previewed finished films, making sure that Hollywood toed the Roosevelt line. That position was articulated in *The Government Informational Manual for the Motion Picture Industry*. For every film, the producers should begin with the question, "Will this picture help win the war?" The mandate was

that the industry would make movies that showed Americas fighting a "people's war" to create a liberal, internationalist, democratic "new world" order.

Films should show Americans pulling together for the war effort—civilians giving up their seats on trains and buses to servicemen and conserving gas and rubber. In the America of the BMP censors, there were no class, religious, ethnic, gender, or racial divides. Everyone read from the same civic hymnal. And in the world of the BMP censors, America's allies shared their values. Britain was a classless society, China was efficient, and the Soviet Union was, in its own peculiar way, democratic.

With so many of the other leading men in the service, John Wayne found himself in a position to give shape to the BMP's ideals. He showed what a BMP's leading man looked like, how he acted under pressure, what values he prized, and what virtues he extolled. He became a one-man propaganda machine. Not only did he believe in the BMP message; he *was* the message. In more than a dozen wartime films, John Wayne represented the triumph of good over evil, justice over injustice, and democracy over fascism. On the sliver screen he battled for "the American way" in Asia, Europe, and America. In film after film, playing a pilot, a sailor, a GI, a Seabee, a steel worker, or a cowboy, he became the cinematic icon of World War II.

The creation of the image began with *Flying Tigers*, Republic's first major war film. *Flying Tigers* was filmed between May and July of 1942, during critical months of the Pacific war. After the attack against Pearl Harbor, the Japanese had defeated U.S. forces on Wake Island, Guam, and the Philippines; British forces in Hong Kong, Malaya, and Singapore; and Dutch forces throughout the Dutch East Indies. Although the U.S. had fought back effectively in the battles of the Coral Sea and especially Midway, it was clear by the summer that the war against Japan would be a long, slow, painful grind. To steel the country for an arduous slog, *Flying Tigers* centered on the need to sacrifice individual glory for collective victory.

There was nothing original about *Flying Tigers*. Its similarities to Howard Hawks's *Only Angels Have Wings* (1939) are blatant. Both films center

★

above WAYNE LEADS THE TROOPS IN *FLYING TIGERS*, 1942. THE FILM UNDERSCORED AMERICA'S SPECIAL RELATIONSHIP WITH CHINA.

FLYING TIGERS POSTER

Movie poster from the war film, *Flying Tigers*, featuring
John Carroll, Anna Lee, and John Wayne, 1942.

MILITARY APPLICATION

Excerpt from Duke's application to join the Army, 1943.

opposite LEADING MAN WAYNE IN *FLYING TIGERS*, 1942.
THE FILM HELPED SET THE PATTERN FOR WORLD WAR II
MOVIES. JOHN WAYNE PLAYED A TOUGH, HARD LEADER
WHO MOLDS A GROUP OF INDIVIDUALISTS INTO AN
EFFECTIVE COMBAT TEAM.

on a small, tightly-bound group of pilots who, led by a man nicknamed "Pappy," engage in a dangerous occupation, and are threatened by destructive individualism and a beautiful woman. In the case of the *Flying Tigers*, the pilots are part of Colonel Claire Lee Chennault's American Volunteer Group, flying against the Japanese in China in the months before Pearl Harbor.

The major difference between *Flying Tigers* and *Only Angels Have Wings* was the timing. Herbert Yates, head of Republic Pictures, sensed that Americans needed a hero for troubled times, and he served them John Wayne. As the leader of the outfit, Wayne is solid, thoughtful, and compassionate, always ready for both heroic action and teamwork. Duke's performance breathes life into the weak script and hasty production. As the moral heart of the film, the camera focuses on his reactions for virtually every event. In one extended scene, director Davis Miller shoots pilots and nurses listening to the radio broadcast of Roosevelt's war message to Congress. For almost three minutes, the only voice heard is FDR's. Wayne's silent presence, stone-faced and grim, gives power to the president's words.

Flying Tigers also conveyed the BMP's primary message. The Chinese in the film appear modeled after Wang Lung and O-Lan in Pearl S. Buck's *The Good Earth* (1937). They are decent, warmhearted, pro-American allies, polar opposites of the bloodthirsty, robotic Japanese. In fact, even BMP's content censors thought the treatment of the Chinese was "blindly generous." Nothing of the divisions in China or the corrupt inefficiency of Chiang Kai-shek's regime is even remotely suggested.

The film, and especially Duke's performance, struck the proper note with the public. "It is a smashing, stirring, significant film," commented a reviewer for the *Hollywood Reporter*. "John Wayne matches his best performance," added the *New York Times* movie critic. "Mr. Wayne is the sort of fellow who inspires confidence."

The box-office success of *Flying Tigers* and the reviews Wayne attracted encouraged major studios to cast him in starring roles. During the war, MGM, Universal, and RKO all gave him leading parts. Added to these, he made his yearly quota of cheaply produced Republic Westerns and war films, including *In Old California* (1942), *In Old Oklahoma* (1943), *The Fighting Seabees* (1944), *Flame of the Barbary Coast* (1945), and *Dakota* (1945). As a result, there was almost always a John Wayne film playing on American screens.

Most evinced obvious propagandistic messages. In *Pittsburgh* for Universal, for instance, he played Charles "Pittsburgh" Markham, a man whose obsession for success overrides his basic

WAYNE AND J. M. KERRIGAN IN *THE FIGHTING SEABEES*, 1944. THIS FILM, ALONG WITH OTHER WAR FILMS, WOULD HELP SOLIDIFY WAYNE'S PLACE AS AN AMERICAN HERO.

humanity. To reach the top of the steel industry he abandons the woman who loves him (Marlene Dietrich) and the partner who supported him (Randolph Scott). But his single-minded drive and blinding ambition eventually destroy him, culminating in a fall as spectacular as his rise.

World War II inspires Pittsburgh to forgo his selfishness. Once again he rises to the summit of a steel company, but not at the expense of personal relationships. He realizes that unity on the home front is as important as teamwork on the battlefield.

The BMP staff was delighted by the film. A preachy epic of the steel and coal industry containing numbing semi-documentary sections on making steel and the by-products of coal, *Pittsburgh* was exactly the sort of educational propaganda that the newspapermen at the BMP admired. "*Pittsburgh* succeeds in making many excellent contributions to the war information program," commented a staffer, judging it "one of the best pictures to emerge to date dealing with our vital production front."

But what pleased the government did not always please movie reviewers or excite the public. They wanted to see Wayne and Scott battle for the love of Dietrich and engage in another epic slugfest, as they did at the end of in *The Spoilers* (1942). They were not drawn to filmmaking by the collective efforts of New Deal newspapermen and earnest Hollywood directors. In truth, BMP was often blind to what made effective propaganda.

Even with the tepid reception of *Pittsburgh*, John Wayne emerged from the first full year of the war a major star. Fittingly, he was beginning to receive star treatment. Director Richard Fleischer recalled being taken on a tour of RKO Studios when he first arrived in Hollywood toward the end

of the war. Every soundstage on the lot was buzzing with activity except one. There, small groups of employees were lounging about conversing in subdued tones. Fleischer soon learned that the problem was that the film's star was taking an unusually long time in the toilet, so everyone had to wait.

Eventually Duke emerged, striding on the set, according to Fleischer, "Big as life. Big as all outdoors. Big as the wheat fields of Kansas, the oil fields of Texas. America's hero." But reflecting on the moment decades later, the director wrote, "What I had witnessed was a display of unadulterated, raw power. Who else could halt production for hours, at a great cost to the studio, by peristalsis alone?"

John Wayne had become a man whom other people treated differently. During the war, leading ladies began to flirt with him, requesting his services even after the end of the day's work. Joan Crawford, notorious for bedding her leading men, made a play for Wayne. But he was married, or at least not interested.

And besides, he was still seeing Marlene Dietrich on the side. That affair eventually ran its course—both cared much more deeply about their careers than each other—but not before Wayne left his wife Josie. Separated from his wife and children for long stretches, he lived like a bachelor, enjoying nights of drinking and card playing with

---

★

---

opposite WAYNE AND MARLENE DIETRICH REUNITE ONCE AGAIN ON-SCREEN IN *PITTSBURGH*, 1942. IT WAS THEIR THIRD FILM TOGETHER, BUT THE WORDY SCRIPT LACKED THE PASSION AND FIREWORKS OF THE OTHER TWO MOVIES.

relationship was as fun-loving, passionate, and volatile as Chata herself. Wayne thought he wanted to spend the rest of his life with her. In the summer of 1943, Josie formally separated from Wayne, and within a few years they were granted a divorce and he married Chata.

His personal problems had no effect on his professional life. Throughout 1943, 1944, and 1945, his movies attracted hundreds of millions of viewers. Americans grew accustomed to watching John Wayne attack Japanese positions in a bulldozer (*The Fighting Seabees*), outfighting a few Western gunslingers (*Tall in the Saddle*), or returning to the Philippines for some unfinished business (*Back to Bataan*). His furrowed brow, cold hard stare, and warm open smile became as recognizable as Bogart's grimace or Gable's leer. Wayne's face, voice, and walk became immediately recognizable across the United States and wherever American troops were stationed.

Even John Ford returned from the war to make a movie with him. The film, based on William L. White's bestseller, was *They Were Expendable* (1945), the story of the experiences of the men of a squadron of PT boats during the months between the Japanese assault of the Philippines and the surrender of Bataan. A bleak period in the Pacific war, when everyone except General Douglas MacArthur

Ward Bond and other friends, and having a few brief affairs.

Earlier on a trip to Mexico City with a party of friends, he had met Esperanza "Chata" Bauer, a woman with a love for the nightlife, a definite reputation, and a combustible temper. Duke fell in love with her and brought her to the United States. By 1943, Chata was living in the Chateau Marmont on Sunset Boulevard as Wayne's mistress. Their

was expendable, the film was a tribute to the sailors who had sacrificed their lives to hold the line in the Philippines while the United States prepared to go on the offensive. Seldom had American forces been treated so reverently in a film. For instance, in the scene of MacArthur's evacuation of the Philippines, shots of the general are accompanied by "The Battle Hymn of the Republic."

The timing of the film was critical. It was shot from March to June 1945, and released just before Christmas. Although VE-Day occurred during production, the end of the Pacific war was not in sight. The fighting on Iwo Jima and Okinawa had been brutal, and the invasion of Japan was set for November 1, 1945. Therefore, when the film was in production, BMP officials assumed that its message of the heroism of sacrifice and service would strike the right note with viewers. The acting, lighting, and score of the film suggested a passion play.

Yet the war was over by the time the film was released, and its moral earnestness had little appeal for Americans weary of the war and war movies. Critics were kind to the film. Bosley Crowther of the *New York Times* wrote, "It is in no wise depreciatory of [*They Were Expendable*] to say that if this film had been released last year—or the year before—it would have been a ringing smash. Now, with the war concluded and the burning thirst

for vengeance somewhat cooled, it comes as a cinematic postscript to the martial heat and passion of the last four years." For the Christmas season of 1945 Americans wanted *The Bells of St. Mary's* and *Spellbound*, not a paean to sacrifice.

But in war or peace, by the end of 1945, they still wanted John Wayne. The war had made Duke a star, pushing him to the top of his profession. There he would remain for the rest of his life—and after.

---

opposite WAYNE AND ESPERANZA BAUER AT THE CLUB TROCADERO, HOLLYWOOD, CALIFORNIA, DECEMBER 13, 1945. *above* MOVIE ART FEATURING WAYNE IN *THEY WERE EXPENDABLE*, 1945. THE FILM HAD EVERYTHING BUT GOOD TIMING.

CHAPTER SIX

SADDLE UP

"LINE 'EM UP AND HEAD 'EM NORTH, PILGRIM."

At the end of WWII, most critics and John Wayne fans did not really regard Duke as an actor. His style was so perfectly natural, his character so charmingly consistent, that it just seemed he was playing himself in front of the camera. His name might change from film to film, but he was always John Wayne on the screen.

After the war, he returned to traditional John Wayne roles, going back to Republic for several Westerns. The first, *Dakota* (1945), was like the others he had made during the war. The second, *The Angel and the Badman* (1947), was a bit more ambitious. Teamed with Gail Russell and Harry Carey, Wayne gives

---

opposite A GRITTY WAYNE STARS AS ROBERT MARMADUKE HIGHTOWER IN
3 GODFATHERS, 1948. AGE ADDED LINES TO HIS FACE AND WEIGHT TO HIS
PERFORMANCES.

up his gun and a life of violence for the love of a Quaker. Duke's other two films of the period were made for the RKO studio: *Without Reservations* was a screwball comedy with the aging Claudette Colbert, and *Tycoon* (1947) was a lackluster, convoluted adventure film of empire building in the Andes. Although both efforts enjoyed modest box-office success, they were panned by the critics. *Without Reservations* demonstrated that both the classic screwball comedy and Colbert's career

as a cute ingénue had run their course. And as the influential reviewer James Agee observed of *Tycoon*, "Several tons of dynamite are set off in this movie; none of it under the right people."

John Wayne's career was drifting. Unchallenging roles in undistinguished films left him artistically bored and concerned about his future in Hollywood. His longtime secretary Mary St. John recalled that he had begun to worry that he was getting too old to play the handsome leading man, and he had never played anything else. He had never been a character actor, and at the age of forty-one, it was difficult to believe that he ever would. Perhaps he could produce or direct, he thought.

Then, for a second time, John Ford came to the rescue.

In late 1947, John Wayne returned to Monument Valley with Ford. Both men needed a hit. Wayne wanted to break out of his career of Republic Westerns and RKO's secondary productions, and Ford was desperate to recoup some of the money his Argosy production company lost on *The Fugitive* (1947). They each needed a sure bet, and there nothing surer at the time than a John Ford/John Wayne Western shot in Monument Valley.

The film, *Fort Apache*, was based on the James Warner Bellah short story "Massacre," which had been published in the *Saturday Evening Post*. A master at adapting and editing, Ford retained the best and discarded the worst of Bellah's tale. The result almost had the smell of campfires and saddle leather, and the look of a dusty western post.

In *Fort Apache*, Lieutenant Colonel Owen Thursday (Henry Fonda), like General George Custer, leads his men into a trap in which virtually everyone is massacred. It is an act of singular ineptness and stupidity, one that crosses over into suicidal arrogance. Yet the film stands as a tribute

to the army in the West, and, by extension, the American military forces in World War II. Two factors save the film from being a wholesale condemnation of the army and its leadership. The first is the loving details of post life. From the hard drinking and the training of troops to the niceties of delivering calling cards and the etiquette of post dances, every detail contributes to Ford's vision of an ideal, holistic community.

The other saving grace is Captain Kirby York (John Wayne), the second in command. York is versed in western warfare and respectful of Native Americans. He cares about his men—not promotion, glory, or fame. The post is his life, not a stepping stone. In short, he is the ideal officer.

Yet, as the film's colead, the role challenged Wayne.

During the previous decade Fonda had given form and substance to Ford's artistic vision, from *Young Mr. Lincoln* (1939), *Drums Along the Mohawk* (1939), and *The Grapes of Wrath* (1940) before the war to *My Darling Clementine* (1946), *The Fugitive* (1947), and *Fort Apache* (1948) after it. Fonda was the recognized artist, the actor's actor, and his liberal sensibilities and man-of-the-people persona perfectly matched John Ford's. Duke was fine playing an innocent gunman without many lines in *Stagecoach*, filling a secondary role in *The Long*

opposite WAYNE WORKING WITH DIRECTOR JAMES EDWARD GRANT ON THE SET OF *THE ANGEL AND THE BADMAN*, 1947. WAYNE WOULD STAR AND PRODUCE THE FILM. GRANT IS BETTER KNOWN FOR HIS WRITING THAN HIS DIRECTING SKILLS.

SADDLE UP

Voyage Home, or making Robert Montgomery seem even more noble in *They Were Expendable*—but in Ford's eyes, Duke was no Henry Fonda.

In *Fort Apache*, Thursday was the more theatrical part. Fonda moved through the film like a bristling peacock, insulting everyone, demeaning his command, and blindly pushing toward disaster. As scripted, York is little more than a second banana, called upon to stand straight, give good advice, and then follow orders. But Wayne gave the part life. His silent reactions to Fonda's jeremiads demonstrate that Duke could say more by saying nothing than anyone in Hollywood.

As a result of his powerful performance, his controversial last lines are believable. In the scene, set years after the death of Thursday, a group of reporters ask York about his former commander. "No man ever died more gallantly. Nor won more honors for his regiment," York says. Then, looking at a heroic painting entitled *Thursday's Charge*, York remarks that it is "correct in every detail." There was no irony in the message. York was not protecting Thursday's legacy as much as he was defending the collective memory of the regiment. Of the men who died with Thursday, he adds, "They aren't forgotten, because they haven't died. They're living ... And they'll keep on living, as long as the regiment lives ... The faces may change, and the names, but

they're there, they're the regiment, the regular army, now and fifty years from now."

Coming as it did on the heels of World War II, *Fort Apache* sent exactly the message to the American people that Ford intended. "It's good for the country," Ford said of York's defense of Thursday. "We've had a lot of people who were supposed to be great heroes, and you know damn well they weren't. But it's good for the country to have heroes to look up to."

Fort Apache came at a perfect time for Wayne's career. Although critics failed to discern the significance of the film, they recognized its mass appeal. It was a solid box office success, a powerful movie, and a clear demonstration that John Wayne did not have to win the heart of a leading lady to stand out in a film. Although Ford still did not consider him in the same class as Fonda, Duke was narrowing the gap.

Beyond Ford, Wayne was expanding his roles. Howard Hawks's *Red River* (1948) was shot prior to *Fort Apache*, although its release was after Ford's film due to legal complications. But it was as important as *Stagecoach* for Wayne's career. "It was the first time I felt like a real actor," he later said. His role as Tom Dunson had several challenges. To begin with, the character ages almost fifteen years from the start of the story to the end, and, for

---

⭐

opposite COLEADS WAYNE AND HENRY FONDA IN *FORT APACHE*, 1948. THE FILM DEMONSTRATED WAYNE COMING INTO HIS OWN AS AN ACTOR.

the first time, Duke had to play a man older than himself. But even more demanding, he had to create a frontier Ahab, a man so ruthlessly driven and single-minded that he lived on the edge of madness. The role forced Duke to dig deep into his soul to breathe life into the fictional cattle baron.

Based on a novel by Borden Chase about the first cattle drive along the Chisholm Trail, the story is deceptively simple. After fourteen years of building his herd in the wilderness of southwest Texas, Dunson and his men drive the cattle north to the railhead at Abilene, Kansas. Along the way they confront Native Americans and outlaws, wide rivers and parched land, and, worst of all, themselves. Dunson drives his men harder than the steer, forcing them to their physical limits and beyond. Finally, his men are led into mutiny by Matthew Garth (Montgomery Clift), as close to Dunson as a son. Though Dunson swears revenge, the two are reunited after a brutal fight in Abilene.

The film has the feel of the open range. Instead of Ford's majestic Monument Valley, Hawks's landscape is a threatening, dreary expanse, a place where men could get killed in a stampede or a Native American attack, or just bored to death by a constant diet of beef and sitting high in the saddle sixteen hours a day.

Hawks conveyed the interior as well as the exterior West, the mettle of the men who built empires on it as well as the look and feel of it. As a result, *Red River* rises to the level of an American epic. Explaining his role, Duke said, "I was playing [Charles] Laughton's part in *Mutiny on the Bounty* in *Red River*. It's just the story of *Mutiny on the Bounty* put into a Western." Hawks suggested it was that and more, commenting that the epic Western was "America's guiding historical myth, our cultural equivalent of the Trojan War and the exodus from Egypt."

Red River demonstrated that there was an audience for adult Westerns. It finished second on *Variety's* list of top moneymakers for 1948, grossing $4,150,000 in domestic rentals. As often has been the case with Westerns, however, contemporary critics undervalued the film. To be sure, they liked it, and they praised Wayne's performance, but they missed its depth and significance. "It may seem a hyperbolic claim," film scholar Gerald Mast wrote, "but no star in the history of film other than John Wayne could play [his] role in *Red River* and make it mean what it does and make the story mean what it does." No one knew better than Hawks the difficulty of Wayne's role. "We were walking a tightrope in telling a story like that," he said. "Are you still going to like Wayne or not?" Audiences answered with a resounding "yes."

Certainly John Wayne's performance impressed the leaders of the industry. But not all his roles reflected his standing. In 1948 and 1949 he starred in three films: *Three Godfathers* (1948), *Wake of the Red Witch* (1949), and *The Fighting Kentuckian* (1949). *Three Godfathers* was a John Ford remake of a 1936 MGM film that had been a remake of a silent movie. A religious allegory that passed as a Western, the film was shot in Death Valley and dedicated to the memory of Harry Carey who had passed away in 1947.

It was a difficult shoot, made more so by the brutal heat of Death Valley and Ford's quarrelsome mood. From the start of production he abused Harry Carey Jr. who had been following his father's footsteps since 1946. Wayne told the young actor that Ford was "only mean to people he really liked." But no one enjoyed the experience.

opposite WAYNE PLAYING AN OLDER VERSION OF HIS CHARACTER, TOM DUNSON, WITH MONTGOMERY CLIFT IN *RED RIVER*, 1948. IT WAS, HE SAID, THE FIRST TIME HE FELT LIKE A REAL ACTOR.

The sentimental film, however, has poignant moments. The Technicolor work by cameraman Winton Hoch was stunning, and the performances by Wayne, Pedro Armendariz, and Carey, are touching. Yet *Three Godfathers* fell just short of being a solid critical or commercial success.

Wake of the Red Witch and *The Fighting Kentuckian* were products of Republic's back lot and modest approach to moviemaking. Neither was intended to do anything more than return a nice profit, and both did. *Wake of the Red Witch's* plot resembled a cinematic Chinese box. It had narrative flashbacks inside narrative flashbacks, and shifted direction so rapidly that the actors seemed to be confused about the course of the action. But Wayne's performance as Captain Ralls is somehow totally believable and compelling. His ability to excel in low-budget Republic films testified to his superior talent.

When given a topflight script, director, cast, and cameraman, he soared. In the last months of 1948 he returned to Monument Valley with John Ford, Winton Hoch, and a group of the director's regulars to make *She Wore a Yellow Ribbon* (1949), a film on par with *Red River*. In theory, *She Wore a Yellow Ribbon* is based on "War Party" and "The Big Hunt," two *Saturday Evening Post* short stories by James Warner Bellah. But in reality the film was a product of Ford's imagination. He was the artist; Bellah's stories merely the paint. Describing his vision to Bellah, Ford wrote in a stream of consciousness shorthand, "Jim, I think we can make a Remington canvas." He enthused about broad shoulders, wide hats, and narrow hips. He imagined war bonnets and eagle feathers, the sound of bugles, prairie expanses, buttes and mesas, and buffalo. Even without a plot line or a word of dialogue, the film had already taken shape in Ford's mind.

Ford shot the film as he had imagined it. *She Wore a Yellow Ribbon* is a work of art. Its plot is minimal—the story of the last week in the military career of Captain Nathan Brittles (John Wayne) and the life of a western army post. In terms of dramatic action, not much happens. Brittles takes his men out on his last patrol, discovers the bloody results of an Native American attack, and finds a way to peacefully defuse the situation. Unlike his role of Tom Dunson, as Captain Brittles—the name itself is significant—Wayne plays a soldier whose mission is peace. He is a negotiator, settling disputes between men under his command as well as between the army and Native Americans. His strength lies in his determination to prevent destructive warfare and preserve peace.

Like *Fort Apache*, *She Wore a Yellow Ribbon* is a tribute to the army. Into the part of Captain

Brittles Ford wove characteristics and expressions of George Washington, Robert E. Lee, and Douglas MacArthur, three of the men whom Wayne most admired. Consequently, Brittles became the sum of American military tradition: respected by his men, fearless in action but never foolhardy, impetuous, vainglorious, or gratuitously violent. He knows that the lives of his men are his most valuable charge.

Audiences loved *She Wore a Yellow Ribbon* and critics praised it. The sight of Monument Valley in Technicolor was breathtaking, and cameraman Winton Hoch captured its different visual moods.

Prompted by Ford, he even kept the camera rolling during a violent thunderstorm. The image of lightning breaking just above a line of cavalry troops is one of cinema's most enduring. At the 1950 Academy Awards, Hoch won the Oscar for color cinematography. Like the script, however, Hoch's camera work was simply paint on Ford's palette.

Fort Apache and *She Wore a Yellow Ribbon* were companion pieces, studies of a cavalry post and different command styles. The first had more action, and the Thursday-York relationship added tension. The second lacked real conflict or tension but was a

---

above MOVIE ART FEATURING WAYNE, HARRY CAREY JR., AND JOHN AGAR IN *SHE WORE A YELLOW RIBBON*, 1949. CAREY RECALLED THAT DUKE CARRIED THE PICTURE AND STILL FOUND TIME TO ALLOW FORD TO WIN NIGHTLY CARD GAMES IN THE MONUMENT VALLEY CAMP.

wonderful character study. Ford had said his piece, and there was no need for another cavalry film. But the demand for a financial success and the desire to get the green light on a different project closer to the director's heart convinced Ford to make another.

Shot in black-and-white for Republic, *Rio Grande* (1950) lacked the elegance and the artistic sensibility of *Fort Apache* and *She Wore a Yellow Ribbon*. Cinematically, it offered nothing new, relying instead on the Irish comedy routines of Victor McLaglen, the expert horsemanship of Ben Johnson, and the singing of the Songs of the Pioneers. Once again the plot is based on a James Warner Bellah short story, "Mission with No Record," from the *Saturday Evening Post*. Only the introduction of Maureen O'Hara to the cast as Wayne's love added anything novel.

The significance of the film was not so much what was on the screen as the timing of the message it imparted. In late 1950, when the film was enjoying wide success, the U.S. Army had crossed the border into North Korea in pursuit of a communist enemy, and in Washington politicians were debating the viability of moving across yet another border into Red China.

The main plot line of *Rio Grande* concerns a cavalry raid across the Rio Grande River to destroy a band of marauding Native Americans. Without official written orders, Lieutenant Colonel Kirby Yorke (John Wayne) crosses the border into another sovereign country on a search-and-destroy mission. In *Rio Grande*, Ford considered such themes as the impotency of diplomacy, the untenable nature of borders, and the need to go after the enemy. In the first two cavalry films Ford preached peaceful coexistence. In *Rio Grande*, he advocated bold action.

Bold action and strong leadership were the themes of another John Wayne film playing across the country in 1950: *Sands of Iwo Jima*. The film was the idea of Edmund Grainger, the executive producer and a close friend of Wayne's. Initially Duke had no interest. He didn't like the script and it seemed like the sort of movie he had made at Republic during the war. But Grainger convinced him that the Marine Corps was not only behind the project but also believed that a publicity boost was needed at a time when Congress was debating the military branch's future. Finally, after bringing on Wayne's own scriptwriter and obtaining permission to use Camp Pendleton and Marine equipment to give the film a realistic look, Wayne agreed to play Sergeant John M. Stryker.

It was a role he wore as comfortably as an old pair of boots, one for which he had been in rehearsal for twenty years. Stryker was a hard-driving Marine

---

opposite WAYNE AS LIEUTENANT COLONEL KIRBY YORKE IN *RIO GRANDE*, 1950. TEAMING WITH MAUREEN O'HARA, DUKE STARED IN FORD'S FINAL CAVALRY FILM.

102

His Sergeant Stryker—strong, silent, devoted to duty and country—struck just the right chord with viewers and critics. *Sands of Iwo Jima* finished in the top ten moneymakers for 1950 and earned Wayne an Oscar nomination for best actor. Although the award went to Broderick Crawford in *All the King's Men* (a role Duke turned down and called an insult to American values), Wayne took satisfaction in the recognition he had received.

Whether fighting on the frontier or on Pacific islands, John Wayne was front and center on the movie screens across America. Audiences admired him, box office returns were impressive, and even the critics had begun to come around. At the end of 1950, the *Motion Picture Herald*, a trade publication, announced what many already suspected: John Wayne was Hollywood's most popular star. He had come a long way since *The Big Trail*, surviving the failure of a big-screen epic, the ignominy of work in serials, years making B-Westerns on Poverty Row, and more than a decade of starring in films for the lightly regarded Republic. He had benefited from his relationship with John Ford and his availability during World War II. But most of all, he had reached the summit of his profession because he worked harder, listened better, and learned faster than just about any actor in the industry. John Wayne was on top and he deserved to be there.

rifle platoon leader. His personal life was in shambles and he was often misunderstood, but he was devoted to the corps and his men. In the course of the film, he prepares and leads his platoon in the invasions of Tarawa and Iwo Jima. In the process, Wayne created an image of the Marine leader that still pervades American society and culture.

The timing of the film could not have been better. The United States had just entered the Korean War and Americans were looking for cinematic portrayals of military leadership. As during World War II, John Wayne provided the image.

⭐

---

opposite WAYNE AS SERGEANT JOHN M. STRYKER IN *SANDS OF IWO JIMA*, 1949. DUKE RECEIVED AN ACADEMY AWARD NOMINATION FOR HIS PERFORMANCE. *above* MOVIE ART FEATURING WAYNE IN *SANDS OF IWO JIMA*, 1949.

CHAPTER SEVEN

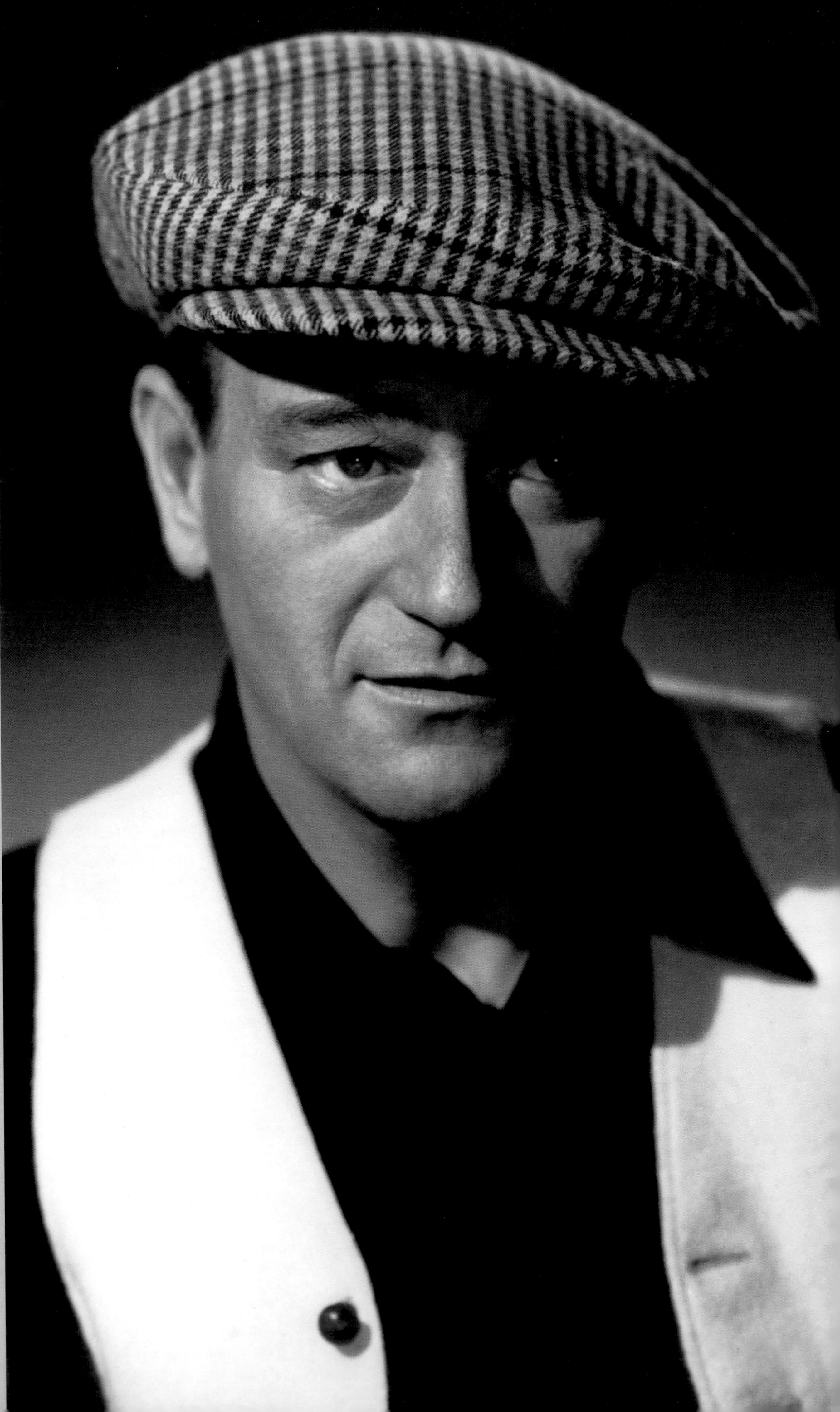

JOHN WAYNE ENLISTS

"IF EVERYTHING ISN'T BLACK AND WHITE, I SAY, 'WHY THE HELL NOT?'"

Judged by any critical standard, John Ford's *The Quiet Man* (1952) was not the finest Ford and Wayne collaboration. But it was unquestionably their most popular. At a time when America appeared riven by international and domestic threats, when the "American way of life" was under attack, *The Quiet Man* was a delightful respite, a feeling that after all the tumult everyone would live happily ever after.

"Well, then, now," Father Peter Lonergan (Ward Bond) began with a cough. "I'll begin at the beginning. A fine soft day in spring it was when the train pulled into Castletown three hours late, as usual, and himself got off."

This opening scene of *The Quiet Man* embraces the viewer, signaling the start of a fairy tale. Set and filmed in Ireland, near Ford's ancestral home, it

--- ⭐ ---

opposite WAYNE IN *THE QUIET MAN*, 1952. IT MAY NOT HAVE BEEN DUKE'S BEST FILM, BUT IT IS HIS MOST LOVED.

is a love story wrapped inside of an even larger love story. If, on the surface, it recounts how Sean Thornton (John Wayne) wins the heart and respect of Mary Kate Danaher (Maureen O'Hara), at a deeper level it explores Ford's feeling for the mythical Ireland of his imagination, a land where no train runs on time, men while away evenings in pubs drinking whiskey and talking revolution, and unalterable traditions govern every aspect of life.

Amazingly, *The Quiet Man* was almost never made. In 1933, when fairy tales were in short supply, the *Saturday Evening Post* published Maurice

Walsh's story "The Quiet Man." Four years later, Ford bought the film rights for $10, promising the writer more if it ever ended up on the silver screen. Over the years he developed the project, even going so far as getting commitments from Duke and Maureen. He also found a screenwriter, Frank S. Nugent, to showcase Wayne and O'Hara as the perfect couple. Ford then surrounded them with an ensemble cast featuring Irish actors.

Yet, even with Wayne and O'Hara and an acceptable script, *The Quiet Man* was a hard sell. For studio chiefs, there was nothing about Ireland that spelled box-office magic, and they were less than enthused that up until the final scene John Wayne would spend all his time playing a romantic lead and doing his best to avoid fighting. Duke was known for many screen qualities, but quietude and pacifism were not among them. In addition, Ford insisted on shooting the film in Ireland, and in the 1940s and early 1950s such expensive indulgences were rare. If he could build a Welsh village near Hollywood as he did for *How Green Was My Valley* (1941) and win an Academy Award, why did he have to transport a cast and crew to Ireland to find an Irish village?

Finally, after a series of rejections and false starts, Herbert Yates, head of Republic Pictures, signed a three-picture deal with Ford's Argosy Pictures. *Rio Grande*, the director's first Republic film, had been a hit. It was everything Yates had desired, so, reluctantly, he approved Ford's Irish lark.

Ford shot the Irish scenes in and around the village of Cong, near Galway, in the summer of 1951. For Duke it was a cozy family affair. All four of his children had small parts in the film, and they enjoyed the opportunity to spend time with their father. Maureen O'Hara recalled that the Wayne kids had a delightful time. "Duke had a great relationship with his kids," she said. "He was wonderful with the boys."

Duke's wife Chata, however, did not always enjoy her time in Ireland. She got along well with O'Hara but seemed jealous of the attention Wayne gave his kids. Her dissatisfaction would only increase over time.

Like Duke, Ford was also surrounded by members of his family. Brothers Francis Ford and Eddie O'Fearna, as well as his brother-in-law Wingate Smith, worked on the film. John Ford's stock company (actors he used repeatedly in his films) were also in attendance: Ward Bond, Victor McLaglen, Barry Fitzgerald, Arthur Shields, Mildred Natwick, and O'Hara.

In his mid-fifties, Ford was heading into the final phase of his career, and he was beginning to question himself. He worried about things—the

---

⭐

---

opposite MAUREEN O'HARA AND WAYNE IN *THE QUIET MAN*, 1952. DUKE TOOK HIS CHILDREN WITH HIM TO SHOOT THE FILM ON LOCATION IN IRELAND.

script, the weather, the Technicolor process, his decisions. Maybe all the nabobs in Hollywood were correct. Conceivably the film did not have enough action. Possibly Wayne could not carry a love story. Perhaps it was, in the end, just a mood piece, a cinematic riff that lacked the completeness of a symphony.

Ford stewed. He became ill. He began to drink—and he was an ugly drunk. Duke also worried about his own role, which was so unlike anything he had ever done. "That was a goddamn hard script," he recalled. "For nine weeks I was just playing a straight man to those wonderful characters, and that's really hard."

When Herb Yates saw the daily rushes back in Hollywood, he added to the second-guessing. He thought the humor was flat, there was no action, and everything looked entirely too green. Yates was sure *The Quiet Man* would be an expensive flop.

It was anything but. The *New York Times* reviewer labeled it "as darlin' a picture as we've seen this year," and *The Quiet Man* was off and running. "Never before, I'm sure, have you seen a movie quite like this one, nor will you ever again, unless you go see it twice or more. Which, incidentally, is what I recommend you do," opined another reviewer. From its opening, *The Quiet Man* was a critical and financial success. Ford received his fourth Academy Award for best director. At the time of the ceremony, he was shooting *Mogambo* in Africa, and Duke accepted the Oscar for him.

Along with *The Quiet Man*, *High Noon* was nominated for best picture. In *High Noon*, the town of Hadleyville is populated by cowards: men and women obsessed by self-interest, devoid of honor, and paralyzed by indecision. Rather than defend what they know is right and stand united against the evil gang descending on their town, they willingly

sacrifice the best among them. Written by Carl Foreman, *High Noon* was seen by many inside and outside the industry as a left-wing morality play, a critique of Hollywood's acquiescence to the attacks of the House Un-American Activities Committee (HUAC). It was a political film from the opening credits to the last scene, and it was treated accordingly. John Wayne despised the movie, maintaining that it portrayed an America foreign to him.

High Noon captured a tempestuous time in the history of Hollywood. In the years after World War II, America found little peace. With the surrender of Germany and Japan the wartime alliance between the United States and the Soviet Union collapsed, and the two nations found themselves on opposite sides of critical geopolitical, ideological, economic, and cultural issues. Termed the "Cold War," it was an ideological conflict between East and West, communism and capitalism, totalitarianism and democracy, the Soviet Union and the United States, and it shaped not only American foreign policy, but also its social and cultural life.

Probably no community in the Cold War was more bitterly torn than Hollywood. In the 1930s and 1940s, many actors, writers, directors, and other members of the film industry were active in left-wing causes, and hundreds joined or were sympathetic to the Communist Party. As early as

---

opposite DUKE ACCEPTS THE BEST DIRECTOR OSCAR FOR JOHN FORD AT THE 25TH ANNUAL ACADEMY AWARDS AT THE RKO PANTAGES THEATRE, 1953. FORD WAS IN AFRICA SHOOTING *MOGAMBO*.

1944, when the United States and the Soviet Union were still wartime partners, a group of conservative members of the film community formed the Motion Picture Alliance for the Preservation of American Ideals (the Alliance). Although John Wayne had not yet joined the Alliance, he agreed with its intention to preserve American beliefs and institutions.

After the war, the Alliance crusaded against communists in the film industry. In 1947, its members invited HUAC to Hollywood to investigate communism, leading to the highly publicized hearings, and eventually trials, of the Hollywood Ten. More hearings followed in the early 1950s. Filmmakers who refused to cooperate with HUAC—those who stood on their First or Fifth Amendment rights and declined to "name names"— were blacklisted from the industry.

Many industry leaders turned timid under the conservative attacks. Not only did they tolerate and enforce the blacklist, they also produced films that were stridently anticommunist. The best, such as *On the Waterfront* (1954), examined the morality of informing and the evils of Stalinist ideology. Such others as *I Was a Communist for the FBI* (1951), *Walk East on Beacon* (1952), and *My Son John* (1952) were inexpensively produced, poorly written B-movie propaganda, in their own way

similar to the Westerns Duke made at Monogram and Republic in the 1930s.

Commenting on the stock quality of the output, film critic Nora Sayre observed, "These films instruct us especially on how American Communists look: most are apt to be exceptionally haggard and disgracefully pudgy. Occasionally, they're effeminate; a man who wears gloves shouldn't be trusted." There were a hundred telltale signs that a person leaned left, but generally closet communists disliked children, mistreated dogs, and were apt to kill one another on the slightest pretext. In fact, as a genre, the films suggested that even without the FBI, American communists would probably end up eliminating one another.

During the late-1940s and early-1950s John Wayne became a fixture on the Hollywood Right. He became president of the Alliance in 1949, a time when the Cold War was reaching a boiling point. During Wayne's four years as president, Senator Joseph McCarthy gained national attention and the Korean War was fought. Although not nearly as strident as other members of the Alliance, Duke worked to rid the film industry of communist influences.

Throughout the period, he took roles in films with an anticommunist message. *Big Jim McLain* (1952) was the most blatant example. Duke had recently formed a production partnership with Robert Fellows, a veteran Hollywood producer, and signed a contract with Warner Brothers for a series of pictures. *Big Jim McLain* was Wayne-Fellows' first film. Behind the camera, Duke surrounded himself with men whom he had worked with comfortably in the past: director Edward Ludwig, writer James Edward Grant, cinematographer Archie Stout, art director Alfred Ybarra, and assistant director Andrew McLaglen. Like John Ford, Duke was intensely loyal to friends, and when given control over cast and crew, he gravitated toward buddies.

There was nothing artful or subtle about *Big Jim McLain*. It begins with a long quote from Stephen Vincent Benet's "The Devil and Daniel Webster," whose crucial line is "Neighbor, how stands the Union?" In the film, Jim McLain (Wayne), an investigator for HUAC, provides the answer: The Union stands one and indivisible. That said, it seems threatened from all sides. Accompanied by his partner, Mal Baxter (James Arness), McLain travels to Hawaii to investigate a communist ring bent on destroying American democracy. The communists are a thoroughly unsavory lot—a leader with a foreign accent, an agent with a personality disorder, and thugs willing to beat anyone into submission. Although McLain is able to uncover and thwart

their plot, the communist agents escape punishment by pleading the Fifth Amendment in court.

John Wayne expected that *Big Jim McLain* would arouse controversy, and it did. Bosley Crowther in the *New York Times* complained, "The over-all mixing of cheap fiction with a contemporary crisis in American life is irresponsible

---

above BIG JIM MCLAIN, 1952, WAS JOHN WAYNE'S PRODUCTION COMPANY, WAYNE-FELLOWS', FIRST FILM. DUKE PLAYED THE TITLE ROLE.

and unforgivable." Other liberal reviewers followed the same line, excoriating Wayne for his views of basic constitutional protections and the communist threat. But other reviewers applauded *Big Jim McLain*, describing it as "an angry film" and "a walloping good movie" that would make viewers "boiling mad."

Important for Duke's production company, *Big Jim McLain* was a solid box-office hit, earning $2,600,000 in domestic rental fees. Considering that it was made for just $825,554, it was strong debut for Wayne-Fellows. The film—and his other message films—did not lessen Duke's appeal. If anything, it enhanced it. As he later said, "I was thirty-second in the box office polls when I accepted the presidency of the Motion Picture Alliance for the Preservation of American Ideals. When I left office … somehow the folks who buy tickets had made me number one."

Other films that reinforced his anticommunist message followed. In *Blood Alley* (1955), he teamed with Cathy Grainger (Lauren Bacall) to lead a village of Chinese refugees to freedom in Hong Kong. In *Jet Pilot* (1957), an effort to update the 1939 Greta Garbo comedy *Ninotchka*, he pursues and beds Soviet jet pilot and spy Anna (Janet Leigh) while finding time to compare political philosophies and dart around the skies. And even when his films were not explicitly anticommunist, they extolled the virtues of the United States and preached preparedness. *Operation Pacific* (1951), *Flying Leathernecks* (1951), and *The Sea Chase* (1955) all had political undertones.

The 1950s was a decade of change for Duke. In 1953 his tempestuous marriage to Chata ended in a messy divorce full of charges of domestic violence, adultery, and alcoholism. The marriage had suffered from many problems, but the worst was Chata's emotional instability and drinking. She was jealous of the attention Duke gave to his children and his single-minded focus on his work. Never able to find contentment, she died a few years later

in a tiny hotel room in Mexico City surrounded by empty liquor bottles.

Before his marriage with Chata ended, Duke met Pilar Palette Weldy in Lima, Peru. Although she was more than twenty years younger than Wayne, she was overpowered by his presence. "He was the handsomest man I'd ever seen," she recalled. "I couldn't believe anyone's eyes could be so blue." Duke was equally struck by her grace and quiet charm. They were soon emotionally involved. They married in 1954, the day Duke's divorce with Chata became final. (Duke and Pilar would have three children: Aissa in 1956, John Ethan in 1962, and Marisa Carmella in 1966.)

⋆

---

opposite WAYNE (RIGHT) WITH JAMES ARNESS IN *BIG JIM MCLAIN*, 1952. *above* DUKE WITH HIS THIRD WIFE, PILAR PALETTE, ARRIVING IN LOS ANGELES AFTER THEIR WEDDING IN HAWAII, 1955.

All this time Wayne's career soared. Despite political commitments, the end of his marriage to Chata, and the start of a new relationship with Pilar, he worked continuously, starring in nineteen films during the decade. Some were artistically bankrupt—*Big Jim McLain*, *Jet Pilot,* and *The Conqueror* (1956) head the list. Some were wonderful escapist larks, the sort of films that defined classic Hollywood. *The Sea Chase, The High and the Mighty* (1954), *The Wings of Eagles (1957)*, and *Hondo* (1953) found enormous audiences. Through it all he worked with some of the most popular leading ladies in the industry. During the 1940s he had played second lead to the likes of Marlene Dietrich, Joan Crawford, and Jean Arthur. Now he was the lead, and Maureen O'Hara, Patricia Neal, Lana Turner, Susan Hayward, Janet Leigh, and Sophia Loren received second billing.

Effortlessly he moved across genres. He was matched with a child actor in the delightful *Trouble Along the Way* (1953); held together the ensemble cast in *High and the Mighty*; made the best of such chase films as *The Sea Chase* and *Blood Alley*; and even played out of character in *The Barbarian and the Geisha* (1958).

But he achieved greatness in Westerns. During the decade he starred in two of the finest Westerns in film history: *The Searchers* and *Rio Bravo*.

In the summer of 1955, he returned with John Ford to Monument Valley to make a film based on Alan Le May's novel *The Searchers*, which had first appeared in serial form in the *Saturday Evening Post* as "The Avenging Texans." Le May's story had centered on the search by Martin Pauley and Amos Edwards (changed to Ethan Edwards in the film) for their relative Debbie, who had been kidnapped and adopted as a daughter by the Comanche chief Scar. It's a tale of hardship and revenge, set against the unforgiving land of the Southwest.

Ford and screenwriter Frank S. Nugent retained the basic plot outline but upended the psychological structure of the film. At a moment when race was central to American thinking, Ford placed it at the heart of the film. In their story, not only had young Debbie been kidnapped by Scar; she had been raised to be one of his wives. Obsessed with race and miscegenation, Ethan (John Wayne) is both driven to find and kill Debbie as well as Scar.

Never had Wayne played such a deeply neurotic and unbalanced character. He oozes hatred and becomes the tortured face of American racism. In one scene, Ethan and Martin find several white women who had been captured and raped by Native Americans, and driven mad by the experience. "It's hard to believe they're white," a soldier says. "They ain't white anymore," Ethan replies. As Ethan's face registers absolute loathing, Ford's cameraman does

---

a rapid track-in close-up, momentarily losing focus. The shot is reminiscent of the one in *Stagecoach* that, in 1939, introduced John Wayne as the Ringo Kid. Then, Wayne was Ford's ideal American—rugged, masculine, open, and innocent. Almost two decades later, he stood thirty feet high on-screen as the face of American racism and xenophobia.

Wayne's performance in *The Searchers* is arguably the most brilliant of his career, and it took a toll on him. Harry Carey Jr., Duke's friend who had a role in the film, recalled that *The Searchers* was unlike any other John Ford/John Wayne film. The mood was more serious. Preparing for their first scene together, Carey said, "When I looked up at [Duke] in rehearsal, it was into the meanest, coldest eyes I had ever seen. I don't know how he molded that character. Perhaps he'd known someone like Ethan Edwards as a kid … He was even like Ethan Edwards at dinnertime. He didn't kid around on *The Searchers* like he had done on other shows. Ethan was always in his eyes."

In addition to the depth of the script and the performance of John Wayne, *The Searchers* is one of the most visually stunning films ever made. Shot in Technicolor VistaVision, it captures the beautiful loneliness of Monument Valley. Ford loved the haunting magnificence of the American West, the way it isolated individuals and made civilization seem like a fragile, doomed experiment. The land in *The Searchers* seems biblical, the region east of the garden, a place fit only for outsiders and renegades. It is the perfect physical exterior for Ethan's disturbed interior.

The Searchers was ahead of its time. Although the film enjoyed box-office success, reviewers did not immediately recognize its greatness. They saw it as a standard John Wayne Western rather than an exploration of the American character. Only later would critics hail it as one of the best films ever made. Duke thought it was John Ford's greatest work. And he would name one of his sons John Ethan. Anyone who ever doubted John Wayne's

greatness as an actor needs only to watch *The Searchers* to realize his genius.

Duke continued to be concerned with packaging the right message about America in his films. Toward the end of the 1950s he teamed with director Howard Hawks to make his finest message movie. *Rio Bravo* came at the right time for Duke. He had turned fifty in 1957, and during the previous few years he had made several mistakes in the roles he chose. *Legend of the Lost* (1957) and *The*

---

opposite WAYNE AS THE DESPICABLE ETHAN EDWARDS LOOKS ON AT A NATIVE AMERICAN ENCAMPMENT IN *THE SEARCHERS*, 1956. *above* MOVIE POSTER ART FOR *THE SEARCHERS*. MOST CRITICS CONSIDER IT WAYNE'S FINEST FILM.

Barbarian and the Geisha, while not as bad as *The Conqueror*, had received poor reviews and lagged at the box office. He needed to return to what he did best.

In *Rio Bravo*, Hawks attempted to broaden the traditional Western audience. Along with Wayne and such stock Western actors as Harry Carey Jr. and Walter Brennan, he cast Rat Pack singer Dean Martin and teenybopper heartthrob Ricky Nelson in major roles, along with the sexy Angie Dickinson as the romantic lead. *Rio Bravo* also featured songs by both Martin and Nelson. Fortunately, Hawks did not call on Duke to carry a tune. The new faces and songs were an effort to reach a younger, more varied audience.

But the plot was standard Western fare. It was from start to finish a rebuttal of Stanley Kramer and Fred Zinnemann's *High Noon*. "I didn't like [the] film," Hawks said. "I didn't think a good sheriff was going to go running around town like a chicken with his head off asking for help, and finally his Quaker wife had to save him. That isn't my idea of a good Western sheriff."

In *Rio Bravo,* Sheriff John T. Chance (John Wayne) is on a collision course with a gang of outlaws. After arresting a man for a cold-blooded murder, he has to keep him in jail pending trial. As the murderer's brother and gang descend on the town, Chance is forced to face overwhelming odds. Unlike *High Noon*, however, Chance is not looking for help, but the community insists on getting involved. Aided by a drunken friend, a crippled man, a good-hearted gunslinger, a Mexican hotel operator, and a dance-hall girl, Chance survives the showdown.

Rio Bravo is not a ham-handed anticommunist film along the lines of *Big Jim McLain*. Instead it appeals to the better angels of the American character—the belief in duty, decency, and the integrity of the individual. Although critics once again missed the deeper meaning of the film, it struck a chord with viewers. It was a solid hit, easing Duke's concern about his poorer films.

But by 1960, John Wayne realized that his career had reached an important juncture. How long could he continue to play the role of the leading man who got the leading lady at the end of the film? He was in his fifties, and most leading ladies were in their twenties. Angie Dickinson, for instance, was only twenty-six—half Duke's age— when she finished filming *Rio Bravo*. And Duke had never played character roles. Increasingly he considered moving to the other side of the camera. Now was the time, he thought, to turn full-time to producing and directing.

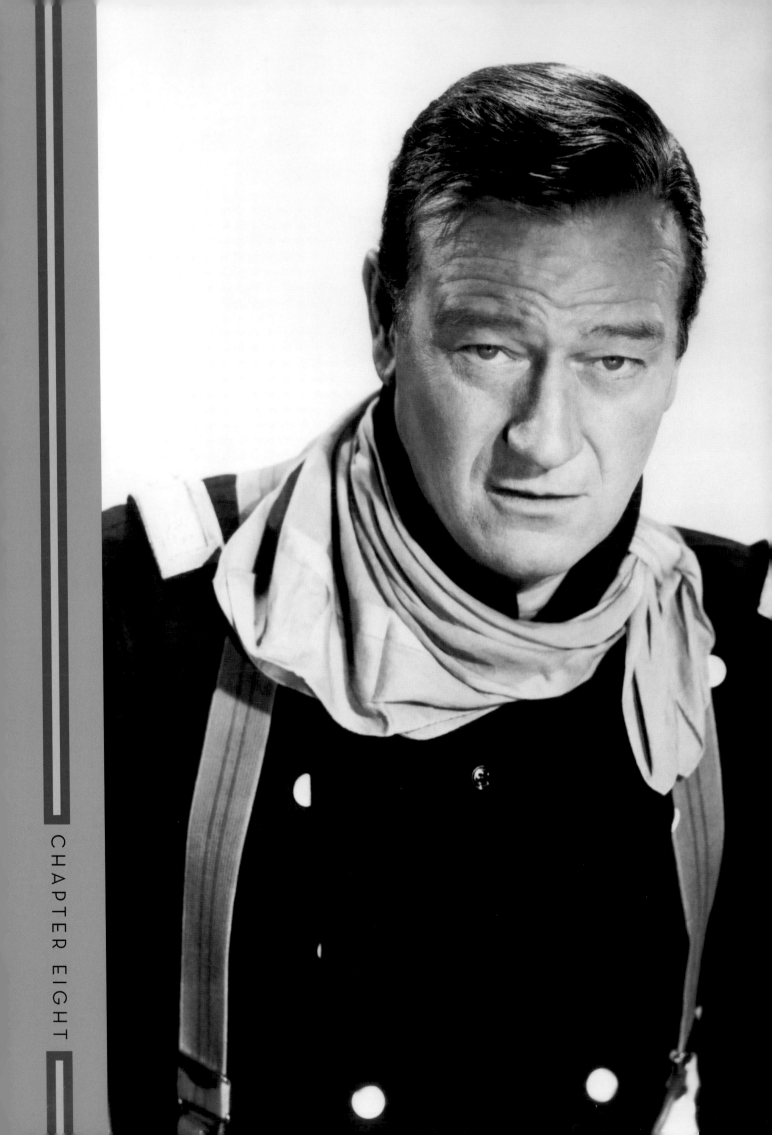

CHAPTER EIGHT

MAKING HISTORY

"THERE'S RIGHT AND THERE'S WRONG. YOU GOTTA DO ONE OR THE OTHER."

The late 1950s was a time of transitions. Some John Wayne had been working toward; others came as complete surprises. He had recently learned that his wife Pilar was dependent on prescription drugs. Though Duke promised to help her kick the addiction, he was starring in John Ford's *The Horse Soldiers* (1959) and did not have the time his wife needed. Without care, she nosedived and attempted suicide. Only then did Duke arrange for the help she desperately needed to overcome her addiction.

Added to Pilar's problems were Duke's financial troubles. Simply put, he was broke. Although he had earned millions of dollars in the movie business, he had devoted little time to managing his money. Instead, he had retained

opposite WAYNE IN *THE HORSE SOLDIERS*, 1959. THE JOY OF WORKING AGAIN WITH JOHN FORD ENDED WHEN A STUNT MAN DIED ON THE SET.

a business manager named Bo Roos, who managed other Hollywood personalities as well. In early 1959, a relatively small, unpaid bill alerted Duke that there was a problem. Pressing Roos for an explanation, he learned that he was broke. He had a house, personal possessions, a production company, and a few virtually worthless investments, but that was it. Through mismanagement, Roos had lost the rest.

The timing could not have been worse, for in early 1959 Duke was making his most significant move into film production. For almost a decade he had been involved in producing films, first with Wayne-Fellows and then with Batjac, his own company. Mostly he had done well. *Islands in the Sky* (1953), *Hondo* (1953), and *The High and the Mighty* (1954), for example, had been solid hits, and a few of the films he produced that he did not act in had also turned a profit. But over the years he had dreamed about a bigger project, which by 1959 had grown into a grandiose vision. He wanted to make a widescreen Technicolor epic that promoted his political beliefs and his love of America. It would be called *The Alamo*.

The dramatic story of the battle of the Alamo had long been a popular film subject. French filmmaker Gaston Méliès produced *The Immortal Alamo* in 1911, and D. W. Griffith supervised the making of *The Martyrs of the Alamo* in 1916. Others followed, including *Davy Crockett at the Fall of the Alamo* (1926), *Heroes of the Alamo* (1937), *The Man from the Alamo* (1953), and *The Last Command* (1955). Walt Disney had even turned out an Alamo saga, *Davy Crockett, King of the Wild Frontier* (1955), starring Fess Parker as Davy and Buddy Ebsen as his sidekick. Duke, however, thought that none of the previous productions did justice to the story. And certainly, none contained the epic vision or packed the political message that he planned.

Duke began developing a script in the late 1940s, and in the early 1950s approached Herbert Yates at Republic about the project. Yates liked the idea, but, as always, wanted to make the film on the cheap. The more Duke explained what he had in mind—a location shoot in Mexico and an elaborate Alamo set—the more nervous the tight-fisted studio chief became. "Who the hell is going to pay to see a picture where all the heroes die?" he asked Wayne. Yates's refusal to back the Alamo project was a major reason Duke cut his ties with Republic, which might have led the producer to approve a different Alamo film, *The Last Command*, at the studio as an act of revenge.

Throughout the 1950s Wayne continued to work on the project. The enormous success of Disney's *Davy Crockett, King of the Wild Frontier*,

which triggered a merchandising craze on anything and everything that had to do with Davy, demonstrated that Americans were fascinated by the battle and would pay to see "all the heroes die." And, as Duke thought about it, he became convinced that in one film he could solve a personal problem and convey his feelings about America.

His personal issues were unavoidable. Simply put, he was an aging leading man, and he believed his future was behind and not in front of the camera. "My problem is I'm not a handsome man like Cary Grant ... who will be handsome at sixty-five," he said. "I may be able to do a few more man-woman things before it's too late, but what

above DIRECTING ON THE SET OF *THE ALAMO*, 1960. ALTHOUGH THE FILM WASN'T VERY WELL RECEIVED, THE PROJECT WAS WAYNE'S LONGTIME LOVE AND HIS FIRST EXPERIENCE AS A DIRECTOR.

then? I *have* to be a director—I've waited all these years to be one. *The Alamo* will tell me what my future is."

With his future hanging in the balance, he labored to find investors and sign a studio deal. Several wealthy Texans, for whom the stand at the Alamo was the central creation story of their state, put up over $5.5 million, and United Artists signed a production deal with Duke and tossed another $2.5 to the pot. By 1958, he was ready to start. Outside of Brackettsville, Texas, Duke's team began to construct a replica of the Alamo.

The movie was crucial for his career, but it was also central to his vision of history. In the popular retelling of the story, Colonel William B. Travis drew a line in the sand at the Alamo and asked the men at the mission to come over to his side and agree to fight—and if need be, die—for the cause of Texas's independence from Mexico. According to legend, in the early-morning hours of March 6, 1836, 184 or more died, including Jim Bowie and Davy Crockett. More than anything else, it was the notion of drawing the line that appealed to Wayne and his generation. To Duke's way of thinking, the failure to stop the aggression of Hitler's Germany in the 1930s was the result of appeasers who refused to draw a line in the sand. The idea that the line had been drawn between East

and West, communism and capitalism, "them" and "us," gave teeth to the containment doctrine in the Cold War. What better vehicle for exploring that line than a film about the Alamo?

Duke threw himself into the making of the film. Not only was he willing to put up what little money he had left, but he also agreed to produce, direct, and star in the film. In the heat of west Texas, he wrestled with endless budget, logistical, script, and set questions; pleaded and threatened to get the best work from cameramen and actors; and still had to find it in himself to play Davy Crockett, the central character in the film. He lost weight, battled dehydration, and sweat so much that he had trouble keeping his hairpiece in place. At times it seemed like every negotiation threatened to lead to a fight. But he stayed at it, working under the blistering sun with temperatures that climbed near 100 degrees, dressing for large parts of the day in buckskins, and worrying constantly that he was going to run out of money before the film was finished. But it was completed and released in the fall of 1960.

For Duke it was more than just another movie. It demonstrated how much his screen image and personal political beliefs had come together. His daughter Aissa commented, "I think making *The Alamo* became my father's own form of combat.

---⭐---

opposite LAURENCE HARVEY, RICHARD WIDMARK, AND WAYNE IN *THE ALAMO*, 1960. WAYNE AND WIDMARK CLASHED ON THE SET.

says, "It ain't our ox that's gettin' gored," Davy responds in true Cold War, anti-Munich fashion: "Talk about whose ox is gettin' gored. Figure this. A fellow gets in the habit of gorin' oxes, it whets his appetite. He may come up north and gore yours."

In another scene Davy extols the virtues of democracy: "'Republic.' I like the sound of the word ... Some words give you a feeling. 'Republic' is one of those words that makes me tight in the throat. Same tightness a man gets when his baby takes his first step, or his first baby shaves, or make his first sound like a man. Some words can give you a feeling that makes your heart warm. 'Republic' is one of those words." And "freedom" is another of those words. As Davy says in the film and Duke believed to be true in life, it meant, "People can live free, talk free, go or come, buy or sell, be drunk or sober, however they choose."

When *The Alamo* was released, reviewers charged it with being too wordy, too political, and too long. *Newsweek*'s film critic described it as "the most lavish B-picture ever made ... B for banal." Nor was it the box-office hit Duke needed to establish a new career as a director. As far as the industry was concerned, he had played a high-stakes game, gambled millions of dollars on a risky venture where the primary action did not occur until the final reel, and barely escaped with the shirt on his back. Other

More than an obsession, it was the most intensely personal project of his career." In most respects, it reveals more about Duke than it does about the battle of the Alamo, more about the politics of the Cold War than the dispute between Texas and Mexico.

Early on in the film Davy (Wayne) takes a stand against aggression. When another frontiersman studies and investors were not anxious to allow him to play another game with house money.

Actually, the film showed that Hollywood was beginning to change, that standards for film content had begun to relax. *The Alamo* seemed like a relic from another era. Other than *The Alamo*, Academy Award–nominated films in 1960 included *The Apartment, Elmer Gantry, Sons and Lovers*, and *The Sundowners*, films that focused on pimps, philanderers, dysfunctional families, and drunks. And, except in *The Alamo*, there were no discussions on-screen about republics, a baby's first step, or freedom—unless it was the freedom to push the cultural borders of expression.

In the end, Wayne was wrong about the potential of the movie. He was also wrong about his imminent decline as a leading man. Perhaps there was not an audience for a wordy epic, but there was still an enormous demand for John Wayne in the films of other directors. The fact that he was battling to keep his weight down, wore a hairpiece, and was no longer the handsome young man he had been in *Stagecoach*, did not matter. He still had the characteristic halting delivery and trademark stride, and he continued to stand for a set of bedrock beliefs about good and evil.

During the first half of the 1960s, while Hollywood struggled to maintain its audience in the age of television, John Wayne was one of the few bankable stars. As such, he was paid handsomely to play bit parts in Technicolor epics that were so grand and long that they made the tiny boxes in American living rooms seem even smaller. In *The Longest Day* (1962), producer Darryl F. Zanuck's homage to the Good War, Duke appeared as Lieutenant Colonel Benjamin Vandervoort, the commander of the 2nd Battalion, 505th parachute infantry regiment, during D-Day and the defense of Sainte-Mere-Eglise. In *How the West Was Won* (1962), the story of the "winning of the west" as seen through the eyes of the victors, he played General William Tecumseh Sherman, legendary Union officer in the Civil War and Commanding General of the Army during much of the American Indian Wars of the 1870s and early 1880s. And in *The Greatest Story Ever Told* (1965), the grandest epic of them all, he played a centurion present at the crucifixion of Christ. Such roles, however, were designed to build his bank account rather than his acting reputation.

Other films during the period were standard John Wayne Westerns, more modest in their budgets, less ambitious in their intentions, and still enjoyable to Duke's fans. *North to Alaska* (1960), *The Comancheros* (1961), and *McLintock!* (1963) were box-office successes and certainly better

---

opposite WAYNE WITH HIS DAUGHTER ON THE SET OF *THE ALAMO*, 1959.

THE LONGEST DAY
STORYBOARD
Illustrated storyboard from the plot of *The Longest Day*, 1962.

THE ALAMO MOVIE TICKET
A movie ticket to *The Alamo*, 1960.

opposite WAYNE AS LIEUTENANT COLONEL BENJAMIN
VANDERVOORT IN *THE LONGEST DAY*, 1962.

received than such non-Westerns as *Hatari!* (1962), *Donovan's Reef* (1963), and *Circus World* (1964).

It is unfortunate that *Donovan's Reef* was the final film in the collaboration between Wayne and Ford. By virtually any yardstick, it is the weakest. By 1962, Ford had begun to lose interest in making movies, and for *Donovan's Reef* he accepted a script that in his prime he would have burned. It's a film of drunken brawls, slapstick humor, and open misogyny.

However, during these years of historical epics, predicable hits, and even a few bad choices, John Wayne also starred in several brilliant historical films that demonstrated the complexity of the American past. Made in 1961 and released in 1962, *The Man Who Shot Liberty Valance* was not a typical John Ford/John Wayne Western. It was a film without the magnificence of Monument Valley, wide western vistas, high-noon gunfights, or even much daylight. Instead, it is a dark, interior film, shot on a studio lot in black and white.

At first glance it seems a meditation on how to confront evil. Liberty Valance (Lee Marvin) is a thoroughly vile gunman who has exercised a reign of terror over the town of Shinbone. The question is: What is the best way to stop a man like Liberty Valance? Tom Doniphon (Wayne) presents the classic Western answer: You fight a gunman with a gun.

In contrast, Ransom Stoddard (Jimmy Stewart), a lawyer from the East, places his faith in the law.

For most of the film, Stoddard pontificates about the law and civilization while Valance relishes in his sheer cussedness, Hallie (Vera Miles) moves emotionally away from Doniphon and toward Stoddard, and Doniphon seems to hang just outside the action. To say the least, Duke was uncomfortable with his role. As he told the director's grandson Dan Ford, "He [John Ford]

had Jimmy Stewart for a shitkicker hero, he had Edmund O'Brien for the quick-wit humor, and he had Andy Devine for the clumsy humor. And Lee Marvin for the flamboyant heavy, and, shit, I've got to walk through the goddamn picture."

Wayne need not have worried. He might not have won the woman, but he won the hearts of the viewers. He, after all, was the ultimate hero in the film. He was the man who shot Liberty Valance. The irony was that Stoddard was given credit for

---

opposite WAYNE AS A CENTURION IN THE EPIC FILM *THE GREATEST STORY EVER TOLD*, 1965. *above* WAYNE WITH VERA MILES IN *THE MAN WHO SHOT LIBERTY VALANCE*, 1962. DUKE DIDN'T WIN THE HEART OF THE LEADING LADY IN THE FILM, BUT HE DID CAPTURE THE HEARTS OF MILLIONS OF VIEWERS.

WAYNE ON SET WITH THE CREW AND JOHN FORD BEHIND THE CAMERA IN *THE MAN WHO SHOT LIBERTY VALANCE*, 1962. DUKE HAD DOUBTS ABOUT HIS ROLE—UNTIL HE SAW THE FINAL CUT.

the kill, which set the foundation of his successful political career.

Although the film received tepid reviews on its release, later critics judged it a masterpiece, Ford's last great film. It was his summing up of the western experience. By the end of the film, the Old West of Tom Doniphon and Liberty Valance had given way to the new West of Ransom Stoddard. The gun had been replaced by the law books, the desert by a garden, and the romance of the gunfight by the reality of railroad legislation. The choice, as Ford frames it, was between understanding the past through heroic legend or prosaic truth. The

newspaper editor makes the final decision, saying, "This is the West, sir. When the legend becomes fact, print the legend."

Producer and director Otto Preminger's *In Harm's Way* (1965) was also a meditation on the American past. Ford took on the Old West, while Preminger confronted World War II. Both were sacred American moments thought generally to represent the greatest characteristics of its citizens. From the "winning of the west" to the "good war" there is a direct line marked by a reverence toward rugged individualism, frontier justice, manly democracy, self-sacrifice, and a love of freedom.

★

---

above IN THE FILM *IN HARM'S WAY*, 1965, DUKE COSTARRED WITH PATRICIA NEAL. THE TWO GOT ALONG PERFECTLY, BUT DUKE WAS IN POOR HEALTH, PLAGUED BY A LOUD, PERSISTENT COUGH. SOON AFTER THE SHOOTING OF THE FILM ENDED, HE LEARNED HE HAD LUNG CANCER.

Just as Ford did with the West, Preminger tried to present a nuanced and realistic look at World War II. Preminger claimed that he was "completely against war" and would never make a movie that glorified it. He rejected the sort of screen heroism of such John Wayne films as *They Were Expendable* (1945) and *Sands of Iwo Jima* (1949).

The result was a film showcasing flawed characters engaged in the Pacific war. The best of the group is Captain Rockwell Torrey (John Wayne), committed to the navy and honor, but also a divorced man who has no meaningful relationship with his only son. From there, the moral fiber of most of the film's characters weakens. Jeremiah Torrey (Brandon de Wilde) is Rockwell's spoiled son; Admiral "Blackjack" Broderick (Dana Andrews) a self-serving officer; Commander Neal Owynn (Patrick O'Neal) a cowardly bully of a politician;

and Liz Eddington (Barbara Bouchet) the sluttish wife of Rock's fellow sailor. But the worst is Commander Paul Eddington (Kirk Douglas), a drunken, homicidal rapist who nevertheless is loyal to Rock and capable of self-sacrifice. Some reviewers compared the film to a soap opera: "a full, lusty slice of life in a time of extreme stress," full of "incidents of adultery, rape, suicide, opportunism and stupidity in the high command."

Beneath the sprawling soap opera, however, is a consistently articulated theme: War is a struggle between order and chaos. In it, lines of humanity blur as it devolves into a struggle between man's lighter and darker angles. Rock represents order, Eddington chaos. Perfectly played by Wayne and Douglas, the characters explore the nobleness and insanity of World War II.

Hollywood insiders predicted that the liberal Preminger and the conservative Wayne would make for fireworks during production. The bald director was a tyrant on the set, famous for saying, "I'm the man with no hair that shoves around people with hair." But during the shooting Preminger attacked the less established actors. He never took on Duke.

But John Wayne had other problems. Throughout the shooting in Hawaii, he was ill, nagged by a hacking cough and often short on energy. Always the professional, however, he turned in a stellar performance. Douglas was amazed by Duke's skill. "[H]e brings so much authority to the role he can pronounce literally any line in a script and get away with it," Douglas said. Still, there was one line that was so excessively corny that Douglas thought even Duke would not be able to pull it off. At one point Wayne had to repeat the John Paul Jones line, "I wish to have no connection with any ship that does not sail fast, for I intend to go in harm's way." Douglas thought, "Oh shit, I've gotta hear him say this line. But you know what? He said it, and he got away with it. Now that's John Wayne."

By 1964 he could read a phone book and keep his audience on the edge of their seats. And he was certainly good enough to hold together a nearly three-hour film like *In Harm's Way*. While some critics charged that he was not a great actor, everyone who worked with him, the professionals on either side of the camera, knew the truth.

But all during the summer of 1964 he felt terrible. He was getting old, he thought. He was fifty-seven, overweight, and drank and smoked too much. And the cough made him feel even older. He just couldn't kick it. Finally, after filming *In Harm's Way*, he decided to have a comprehensive physical examination. The examining physician ordered

opposite WAYNE WITH KIRK DOUGLAS IN *IN HARM'S WAY*, 1965. THE STOIC WAYNE AND OVER-THE-TOP DOUGLAS MADE A DYNAMIC IF ODD COUPLE.

more tests, particularly a full battery of chest X-rays. Through all the tests Duke remained unconcerned. He had had what seemed like a hundred exams; they were part of being a major actor.

This all changed when his doctor told him that he had lung cancer. On the morning of September 17, 1964, a surgeon at the Good Samaritan Hospital in Los Angeles removed a golf-ball-sized tumor from the upper lobe of his left lung. Within a week he underwent a second surgery to treat several complications from the first operation, and a few weeks later yet another to remove an obstruction from his chest. For a man who had enjoyed unusually good health, the operations left him scarred, weak, and dependent on occasional help from oxygen tanks.

Through it all, the press was kept in the dark about his diagnosis. When Duke checked out of Good Samaritan in mid-October, he acted like nothing of importance had taken place. Eschewing standard practice of using a wheelchair, he walked out, his head high and a smile on his face, shaking a few hands and exchanging quips with reporters. But once in his limousine he needed supplemental oxygen.

How long could he keep the fact that he had lung cancer secret in a city where virtually nothing was private? His agent and managers told him that if he admitted the truth it would destroy his career.

They insisted that his image was larger than life, that the John Wayne the public knew was an indestructible force of nature. He might get shot on-screen every now and then, but he didn't catch a cold or develop lung cancer. That was for mortal men.

Yet the story was going to come out. Duke decided the best option was to make his own statement and try to control the public relations fallout. On December 29, 1964, he gave columnist James Bacon the exclusive story, confessing that he had undergone an operation for lung cancer. That was the bad news. As for the good news, he said, "I had the big C, but I've beaten the son of a bitch." He was, after all, John Wayne. The undercurrent of his message was that if he could outfight and outshoot any man on-screen, he could defeat the dreaded disease in real life.

His fans accepted his version of events, believed that he had "licked the big C," and sent him thousands of letters and cards. They wished him well and expressed their desire for his quick return to acting. They agreed with actor Robert Stack, who said, "Even with one lung ... [John Wayne] was more man than anyone I know."

After resting a few months, Duke was ready to give his fans what they wanted. He was burning to get on with his second act.

⎯⎯⎯⎯⎯⎯⎯⎯⎯⎯⎯ ★ ⎯⎯⎯⎯⎯⎯⎯⎯⎯⎯⎯

opposite WAYNE LEAVING GOOD SAMARITAN HOSPITAL, LOS ANGELES, OCTOBER 7, 1964. LOOKING LIKE HE DIDN'T HAVE A CARE IN THE WORLD, HIS ACTING ABILITIES PERMITTED HIM TO FOOL THE PRESS.

CASTING A GIANT SHADOW

"THIS KIND OF WAR, YOU'VE GOT TO BELIEVE IN WHAT YOU'RE FIGHTING FOR."

"Screw ambiguity," Wayne once said. "I don't like ambiguity. I don't trust ambiguity." By 1968, when *The Green Berets* came out, Wayne had etched his simplistic political philosophy in stone. He viewed Vietnam as a straightforward conflict. The international communist conspiracy had cast its eyes on Southeast Asia, and the United States had a duty to stop it from succeeding.

"What the hell is happening to this country?" Duke asked after watching antiwar demonstrators at USC—his alma mater—verbally abuse a veteran who had lost his arm in Vietnam. The student movement and associated

opposite WAYNE IN ROME PROMOTING *CAST A GIANT SHADOW*, 1966. WAYNE HELPED ASSEMBLE AN ALL-STAR CAST, INCLUDING KIRK DOUGLAS, YUL BRYNNER, FRANK SINATRA, AND ANGIE DICKINSON, FOR THE PRODUCTION. DUKE STOLE THE FILM DESPITE BEING ON-SCREEN FOR ONLY ABOUT FIFTEEN MINUTES OF IT.

antiwar movement puzzled and disgusted him. A self-made man who had internalized the cowboy ethos of individualism and hard work, he viewed the protestors as spoiled children who had been tricked by radicals into tearing down their own country. Their permissive attitude toward sex and drugs appalled him almost as much as their disdain for authority. He believed Lyndon Johnson's Great Society encouraged this moral decline. "I don't think a fella should be able to sit on his backside and receive welfare," Duke said. "I'd like to know why well-educated idiots keep apologizing for lazy and complaining people who think the world owes them a living."

Wayne's attitude resonated with the people Richard Nixon called the Silent Majority. America was a fractured nation. The building conservative movement desired an end to the racial strife of the Civil Rights and Black Power movements, the campus chaos of the Youth Movement, and the gender upheaval of the Women's Movement. They distrusted intellectuals, yearned for law and order, and preferred stability to more change. Duke became their guiding star, a fixed point in a rapidly shifting firmament.

Wayne's films had long promoted traditional values, a message he was preaching off-camera by the mid-1960s. He stumped for conservative

Republican Barry Goldwater in 1964, and two years later he endorsed Ronald Reagan for governor of California. After knocking out a series of routine pictures that included *The Sons of Katie Elder* (1965), *Cast a Giant Shadow* (1966), and *The War Wagon* (1967), he looked to make another red-blooded, pro-American statement, just as he had in *The Alamo*. Americans needed to know what their sons, brothers, and fathers were fighting for in Vietnam. "I owe it to them," he declared.

Wayne bought the movie rights to Robin Moore's best-selling novel *The Green Berets* in 1965. A letter to Lyndon Johnson helped win the military's cooperation. Finding a distributor proved more difficult. With antiwar protests growing larger, no studio executive wanted to get stuck with a controversial, unpopular picture on their hands. Universal and Paramount rejected the project before Warner Bros. finally agreed to handle it.

At the Pentagon's invitation, Wayne visited Fort Bragg, North Carolina, in 1966 to watch Green Berets being trained. Two months later he visited Vietnam as part of a three-week USO tour (the same length of time his character, Colonel Mike Kirby, would spend in the field). To his amazement, many Vietnamese knew him. "Number one cowboy, number one cowboy!" they shouted. More important, American GIs knew him. "Hello, soldier," he told each one he met. "I'm John Wayne and I just want you to know a hell of a lot of folks back home appreciate what you're doing."

Wayne shot *The Greet Berets* at Fort Benning, Georgia, over the summer and fall of 1967. Thunderstorms and unseasonably cold weather plagued the production. Duke pushed his aging body despite shortness of breath, bouts of coughing, and an aching back and legs. The burden of both directing and starring in the picture was too much; veteran director Mervyn LeRoy took over directing duties at Warner Bros.'s insistence.

Robin Moore's novel characterized South Vietnamese soldiers as corrupt and ineffective, and included detailed (and approving) passages on the use of torture. Duke removed these inflammatory elements, reshaping the story into a flag-waving celebration of American soldiers and their allies. The Green Berets arc top physical specimens fluent in a dozen languages and raring for action. The South Vietnamese are crack troops who work hand in glove with their American mentors.

The Green Berets embraces B-Western morality, reducing the conflict to white hats versus black hats, freedom lovers versus vicious communists. Duke's presence alone signals the survival of the cowboy hero. Vietcong guerillas whoop and holler like the Native Americans of *Stagecoach* as they

attack "Dodge City," the Americans' nickname for their camp. As in Duke's B-movies, the Green Berets' mission is to tame savages and civilize the wilderness, a point made through Colonel Kirby's insistence that his men bulldoze a swath of forest in order to improve the camp's defenses. Surrounded by enemies, Dodge City becomes another Alamo, another stride in the onward march of freedom.

★

---

above DUKE DIRECTING DURING THE FILMING OF *THE GREEN BERETS*, 1968. THE SHOOT DRAINED WAYNE'S ENERGY SO MUCH THAT HE HIRED OUTSIDE DIRECTORS TO EASE THE BURDEN.

Wayne also updated the World War II film genre, with the cunning, devious, militaristic Vietcong standing in for the cunning, devious, militaristic Japanese. The second half of *Green Berets* repeats a formula Wayne mastered in *Flying Tigers* and *Sands of Iwo Jima*, and also appears in such films as 1967's *The Dirty Dozen*—sending a small, diverse unit to accomplish a concrete mission to hasten the end of the war. In this case Wayne leads his men against desperate odds to kidnap a turncoat Vietnamese general.

World War II–era combat films typically featured an alienated soldier who needed to be integrated before his unit could achieve success. Journalist George Beckworth (David Janssen) plays that role in *The Green Berets*. At first he epitomizes the snooty, liberal elitist who, as Spiro Agnew argued, wrote garbage best suited for the bottom of a birdcage. He arrives in South Vietnam wearing clumsy safari gear, unable to carry his clunky suitcases. His time in-country pulls him toward Colonel Kirby. He helps soldiers load a mortar when Fort Dodge is attacked and, beginning the next morning, starts toting a rifle. When Beckworth returns for a second tour, he is clad in army green and carries a duffel over his shoulder. No longer a civilian, he has become a journalist-soldier determined to share the truth about Vietnam.

With its over-the-top militarism, good-versus-evil sensibility, and silly mistakes (Pine forests in Vietnam? The sun setting in the east?), *The Green Berets* was easy to mock. Renata Adler of the *New York Times* called it "so unspeakable, so stupid, so rotten and false in every detail that it passes through being fun, through being funny, through being camp, through everything and becomes an invitation to grieve, not for our soldiers or for Vietnam … but for what has happened to the fantasy-making apparatus in this country … It is vile and insane. On top of that, it is dull." More succinctly, the *New Yorker* called it "a film best handled from a distance and with a pair of tongs." *Green Berets* was obvious propaganda—no more and no less than the films Wayne made during World War II—but this time critics believed he was on the wrong side of history.

Duke didn't care. "I've been to Vietnam, and I've talked to the men there, and I don't have the slightest doubt about the correctness of what we are doing," he told an interviewer. "It's my country, right or wrong, and pure as the driven snow. Americans will be the heroes of *The Green Berets*." If anything, he saw the attacks as confirmation that his opponents were unpatriotic and out of touch. Wayne had the last laugh, as *The Green Berets* raked in millions at the box office. The silent majority had spoken. Wayne was a hero to the working class and cultural conservatives. His uncluttered view of the world filled a need in a society that appeared to be coming apart at the seams.

Contrary to Wayne's wishes, *The Green Berets* widened rather than healed national wounds. Antiwar protests grew larger and angrier during the production. A half-million demonstrators filled Central Park in mid-1967, chanting, "Hey, hey, LBJ, how many kids did you kill today?" In that same year, Jane Fonda, the daughter of Duke's friend Henry Fonda, characterized American soldiers as chilled-out men who disregarded authority and smoked pot. That, along with her 1972 trip to Hanoi, incensed Duke. "Can't she see she's being used by those Commies?" he sputtered. The January 1968 Tet Offensive further polarized Americans on the eve of *The Green Berets'* release. Beloved CBS

★

---

opposite WAYNE AS COLONEL MIKE KIRBY TAKING COVER IN THE *GREEN BERETS*, 1968. ALTHOUGH A BOX-OFFICE SUCCESS, THE CONTROVERSIAL FILM CAUSED SOME TO LABEL WAYNE AN EXTREME RIGHT-WINGER.

anchor Walter Cronkite was among the many who thought the war unwinnable.

———————— ☆ ————————

Duke took a break from filming *Cast a Giant Shadow* to don his public uniform for an appearance on *The Dean Martin Show*. Clad in a red flannel shirt, leather vest, and white neckerchief, he rode a horse on stage for a skit that veered into mawkish sentimentality when Martin asked about

Wayne's hopes for his new daughter, Marisa. "I'd like her to know some of the values we knew as kids, some of those values that too many people these days are thinking are old fashioned," he replied. Looking straight at the camera as he delivered his homily, he continued, "Most [of] all, I want her to be grateful, as I am every day of my life, to live in these United States."

In 1968, Duke made his first of four cameos on a very different program, the antiestablishment comedy *Laugh-In.* This time he walked on stage wearing a gray suit and a brown tie. The audience tittered as he held up an oversized red, white, and blue artificial flower, bowed stiffly, and, imitating cast member Henry Gibson's shtick, deadpanned a poem: "The Sky—by John Wayne. The sky is blue, the grass is green. Get off your butt and join the Marines." Rather than retrace his steps, he exited by walking through the set wall behind him.

Wayne was fully aware of his public persona as a brutish, right-wing cowboy. Just seeing him without a hat seemed as disorienting as seeing the Statue of Liberty raising a candelabra. He was content to play along, keeping his career alive by giving audiences what they wanted while at the same time mocking his own iconic status.

Rooster Cogburn, the one-eyed, drunken, paunchy marshal from Charles Portis's 1969 novel *True Grit,* offered the perfect vehicle for a sixty-one-year-old cancer survivor seeking an exclamation mark for his career. Rooster's quest to avenge the killing of fourteen-year-old Mattie Ross's father placed him within the Wayne tradition of mysterious gunslingers, free from familial attachments, who use violence to restore law and order. At the same time, Rooster's overblown pride (a trait suggested by his name), selective ineptitude, and helplessness in the face of young Mattie's prim determination

make him a comic figure Wayne could use to lampoon his own larger-than-life image.

Like Tom Doniphon in *The Man Who Shot Liberty Valance,* Rooster is a holdover from a bygone era. Wayne plays him as uncomfortable in civilization, squirming on the witness chair in Judge Parker's court and unwilling to mollify his ex-wife by settling down to become a shopkeeper. Modern-day bureaucracy confuses him; he prefers the good old days, when right was right and wrong was wrong. Rooster's complaint that rats had more rights than rat catchers reflected Wayne's distaste for a society that showed more concern for the accused than for crime victims.

This sense of loss pervaded 1960s Westerns as the fresh-faced civilizers of *The Big Trail* and *Westward Ho* were replaced by grizzled, haunted victims of civilization's spread. The protagonists of *Butch Cassidy and the Sundance Kid* (1969) and *The Wild Bunch* (1969) are ruthlessly hunted down by the forces of modernity. They exist not in the West's primordial days, but rather in its sunset years, a time when automobiles coexisted with horses and the frontiersman was a relic. In casting General Custer as the villain, *Little Big Man* (1970) asked whether the Western hero ever really existed. Clint Eastwood's Monco character in *A Fistful of Dollars* (1964), *For a Few Dollars More* (1965), and *The*

⭐

opposite BY 1965, WHEN HE APPEARED ON *THE DEAN MARTIN SHOW,* WAYNE WAS WILLING TO PLAY TO TYPE. FOR THIS SKETCH, HE MOUNTED A HORSE AND SPOKE TO DEAN ABOUT PATRIOTISM AND HIS HOPES FOR THE AMERICAN FUTURE.

Good, the Bad, and the Ugly (1966) is a consummate antihero, a scruffy good-bad guy whose ethics shift according to what is most advantageous for him at a given moment.

Wayne jumped when producer Hal Wallis offered him the role of Rooster, a character who, in Duke's eyes, was both timeless and timely. Henry Hathaway, who directed Wayne in *Shepherd of the Hills* (1941), *North to Alaska* (1960), *Circus World* (1964), and *The Sons of Katie Elder* (1965) also came on board, as did first-time actor Glen Campbell in

the role of La Boeuf, a Texas Ranger who becomes Rooster's sidekick, and twenty-two-year old television actress Kim Darby, who took the part of Mattie. Campbell, who struggled to carry off the role, couldn't believe his luck. "It was one of the biggest thrills of my life, just to ride on a horse next to John Wayne," he exclaimed. Darby was less impressed. "To tell you the truth, I had no idea [of]… the icon he was," she said.

Duke found Darby an insufferable brat but maintained his professionalism throughout. Their relationship formed the heart of the film as Mattie evolves from a cold-hearted automaton to a moralistic nag to a dependent little girl, while Rooster goes from a drunken misanthrope to a less-drunken paternal figure. Wayne's wide-(one) eyed, broadly comic reactions to Darby's lecturing could have rung false. But the responses feel real precisely because it is John Wayne on-screen. Like Rooster, he, or at least his screen character, has never been talked to in such a patronizing way without drawing a revolver. Rooster can only react with profound amazement.

True Grit's climactic shootout gave Rooster a chance to enjoy a classic John Wayne moment. Train robber Lucky Ned Pepper's (Robert Duvall) gang meets the marshal in an open field. They exchange insults. "I call that bold talk for a one-

eyed fat man," Pepper yells. Rooster's eye bugs. For just a moment he reels in the saddle as if caught by a left hook. Regaining his wit, he retorts, "Fill your hand, you son of a bitch!" He takes the reins in his mouth, yanks his rifle from its holster, and gallops toward the bandits with guns ablaze. And there, suddenly looming in the background, is Chimney Rock, a lonely, flat-topped peak that is the closest thing Colorado has to Monument Valley. Filmed at 9,000 feet above sea level, an altitude that left Wayne gasping between takes, *True Grit* had until this point used beautiful but predictable Rocky Mountain peaks for its landscape. The unexpected introduction of Chimney Rock transforms the confrontation into a retrospective. The fat old man becomes the Ringo Kid, Captain Kirby York, and

---

⭐

---

opposite MOVIE POSTER FOR *TRUE GRIT* FEATURING WAYNE, KIM DARBY, AND GLEN CAMPBELL, 1969. WAYNE THOUGHT THE FILM OFFERED HIM HIS FIRST GOOD ROLE IN YEARS. *above* *TRUE GRIT* COSTARS WAYNE AND KIM DARBY DISLIKED EACH OTHER IN PERSON BUT PRODUCED REMARKABLE SCENES FOR THE CAMERA.

Ethan Edwards as he once again vanquishes his foes and restores order.

"It's sure as hell my first decent role in twenty years," Duke told Roger Ebert. Reviewers who had spent years ridiculing Wayne lavished praise on *True Grit*. "After *The Green Berets*, I thought I'd never be able to take John Wayne seriously again," wrote Vincent Canby of the *New York Times*. Indeed, *True Grit* restored much of the goodwill Wayne had lost among some Americans. Instead of a hawkish culture warrior, he became what Gary Wills called "an impressive anachronism," a powerful if harmless proponent of traditional values. As a sign of his return to favor, people in the movie industry were already talking about him as a lock for an Oscar nomination.

———————— ☆ ————————

Wayne was flying high in late 1969. *Box Office Magazine* had just named him the year's top draw. He was having a wonderful time shooting his next feature, *Chisum*, in the dismal little outpost of Durango, Mexico. It was exactly the kind of one-horse town he loved—isolated, quiet, and exempt from Hollywood's strict union-labor laws. Several years earlier he had shot some of *The Sons of Katie Elder* here, and he later returned to film *Big Jake* (1971), *The Train Robbers* (1973), and *Cahill, United States Marshal* (1973).

The good times got even better when he learned of his Academy Award nomination for *True Grit*. It was his first nomination as an actor since *Sands of Iwo Jima* twenty years earlier. In true John Wayne style, he brushed off the nomination like a fly from his hat. "Hell, I'm honored," he told reporters. "Who wouldn't be? But you can't eat awards, and you sure as hell can't drink them." He was of course thrilled, but it wouldn't do to appear too worried about the approval of his peers.

Wayne was pretty sure he was not going to win. That year's competition was particularly fierce, and many Academy voters saw him as a political troglodyte. Peter O'Toole's performance in *Goodbye, Mr. Chips* pleased him, and he thought Richard Burton was brilliant as Henry VIII in *Anne of the Thousand Days*. He approached the other two nominees, Dustin Hoffman and Jon Voight, with more trepidation. *Midnight Cowboy*, in many ways a refutation of the entire Western myth, was the kind of new-Hollywood production he hated. At a private screening he closed his eyes through some scenes and cringed at others. In the end, however, he agreed that both actors gave astonishing performances. "Whoever thought I'd say good things about a movie featuring a gigolo, a homeless Italian dwarf, and gang rape?" he asked his secretary.

Wayne's nomination prompted groans among some critics. *New York Observer* columnist Rex Reed panned the selection in an appearance on the *Dick Cavett Show*. "I really have the terrible, lurking, poisonous suspicion that John Wayne will win," he moaned. Hipsters in the crowd groaned in sympathy. Reed's animosity confused the genial host, who described his childhood fantasy of being John Wayne. Reed retorted that while he had nothing personal against Wayne, "the fact that he has finally played a smelly old drunk who falls off his horse … is just not a good enough reason to give the man an Academy Award."

———————— ☆ ————————

opposite WAYNE AND DIRECTOR HENRY HATHAWAY DISCUSS THE CLIMACTIC SCENE IN *TRUE GRIT*. COLORADO'S CHIMNEY ROCK LOOMS IN THE BACKGROUND.

By Oscars Day, Wayne had pegged Burton as the favorite. Pros that they were, Duke and Burton agreed to have drinks together after the ceremony no matter who won.

The Dorothy Chandler Pavillion hosted a rare intermingling of old and new Hollywood. Gray-haired titans—Jimmy Stewart, Fred Astaire, and of course Duke—sat alongside a generation that, in the 1930s, would have been lucky to score character-actor roles in Warner Bros. gangster flicks. Hoffman, Elliot Gould, and Jack Nicholson were not exactly classic screen faces. The nominated films were similarly schizophrenic, as bloated costume epics like *Anne of the Thousand Days* and *Hello, Dolly!* competed against such daring efforts as *Easy Rider* and *Bob & Carol & Ted & Alice*.

Hello, Dolly!, *Butch Cassidy and the Sundance Kid*, and *Midnight Cowboy* dominated the early going. Finally it was time for the Best Actor category. Barbra Streisand took the stage in a pillbox hat and a pink dress with a plunging neckline. She joked with the audience as she turned to her left and right, searching for someone to hand her the envelope. Voight fidgeted as Streisand read his name. Burton studied his program as if it were a wine list. Wayne stared at the floor and squeezed Pilar's hand. Streisand opened the envelope and tossed a sassy look at the camera. "I'm not going to tell you," she smirked as the audience laughed.

"And the winner is ... John Wayne for *True Grit*."

Nobody can say what Duke was thinking at that moment. Forty years since *The Big Trail*. Thirty years since *Stagecoach*. Dozens of B-movies. His closest friends, growing old. Maybe he just concentrated on not falling down. He accepted the trophy and kissed Streisand on the cheek. Then, in a most un-John Wayne moment, he dabbed a tear that, with impeccable timing, materialized in the corner of his eye. "Wow," he exhaled in a raspy voice.

Duke pulled himself together. "If I'd have known that, I'd have put that patch on thirty-five years earlier," he joked. He recalled the wit he mustered at previous ceremonies when he accepted "beautiful golden men" on behalf of John Ford and Gary Cooper. "Tonight I don't feel very clever, very witty," he concluded. "I feel very grateful, very humble, and owe thanks to many, many people." After thanking the Academy he remembered a more important group. His eyes catching the camera for a moment, he thanked "all you people who are watching on television." But what to say to the countless fans who believed in a man—and an idea—named John Wayne? He fumbled for words. "Thank you for taking such a warm ... interest ... in our glorious

industry. Good night." Breck Coleman, or the Ringo Kid, or John Stryker, or Rooster Cogburn would have delivered the same speech.

True to his word, Duke shared at least one drink with Burton before returning to the set of his next film, *Rio Lobo*. He arrived to find the cast, the crew, and his horse wearing eye patches. John Ford was there too. "Look at that famous Academy Award winner now," he grumbled after Duke nailed a scene. "He does it in one take. When he worked for me, it took fifty."

Wayne was too happy to be upset. "That Oscar meant a lot to me," he admitted, "even if it took them forty years to get around to it."

———————————— ✪ ————————————

above DUKE WIPES A TEAR AFTER ACCEPTING THE BEST ACTOR OSCAR FROM BARBRA STREISAND AT THE 42ND ANNUAL ACADEMY AWARDS, 1970.

CHAPTER TEN

INTO THE SUNSET

"I HAVE TRIED TO LIVE MY LIFE SO THAT MY FAMILY WOULD LOVE ME AND MY FRIENDS RESPECT ME. THE OTHERS CAN DO WHATEVER THE HELL THEY PLEASE."

Duke was known and loved around the world, with millions of fans and the respect of his peers. And he was lonely. By the early 1970s he felt like a stranger in a strange land. Hollywood was making pictures that offended him. Vietnam was tearing the country apart. Social revolutions had reshuffled race and gender relations.

Wayne was well into his sixties and had ballooned to around 250 pounds—hardly the model of a rugged hero. His body ached from a variety of ills, most recently a dislocated shoulder incurred while filming *The Undefeated* (1969). Good parts were difficult to find even after *True Grit*. Old friends were dead, dying, or over the hill. His marriage to Pilar existed mostly on paper. They

---

opposite WAYNE IN *CHISUM*, 1970. WAYNE WAS STILL A BANKABLE WESTERN STAR, BUT MAKING MOVIES TOOK A TERRIBLE TOLL ON HIS BODY. HIS STEELY GLARE, HOWEVER, REMAINED INTACT.

separated in 1973. Wayne knew he was a relic, but didn't know what to do about it. "Goddammit, I hate getting old," he complained. "You just can't do what you used to do anymore."

Wayne vented his frustrations in a 1971 *Playboy* interview. Contributing Editor Richard Warren Lewis got the grand tour of Wayne's Newport Beach home, stopping to admire the actor's Hopi Indian dolls and the many photos of his eighteen grandchildren. The two chatted through the morning before Wayne drove them in his station wagon to his beloved *Wild Goose*, a converted navy minesweeper that served as his home away from home. Fueled by charbroiled steaks and a bottle of tequila, their conversation continued until sunset. They met again at Batjac's offices a week later to tie up loose ends.

Lewis's concern that Wayne would shy away from controversial areas evaporated with the first question. "How do you feel about the state of the motion-picture business today?" he asked. "I'm glad I won't be around much longer to see what they do with it," Wayne replied. "The men who control the big studios today are stock manipulators and bankers. They know nothing about our business … They're producing garbage."

After that shot across the bow, Wayne unlimbered the big guns when the pair turned to social and political matters. "[Liberals] seem to be quite willing to have Communists teach their kids in school." Native Americans didn't deserve an apology or better treatment because "our so-called stealing of this country from them was just a matter of survival." "Liberal Senators…put far too many barriers in the way of the military." And yes, he was a Nixon man through and through—he cited the president's "reasonableness" as the source of his confidence.

Lewis loved it. Duke being Duke, speaking his mind plain and clear, was sure to sell magazines. One of Wayne's final answers, however, caught him by surprise. "Are you … gloomy about the future of America?" Lewis asked. "Absolutely not," Wayne replied. "I think the pendulum's swinging back. We're remembering that the past can't be so bad. We built a nation on it. We must also look always to the future."

That was John Wayne in 1971, cherishing the past while nodding toward an uncertain future. The movies he made during that period embraced the same spirit. He did not belong in edgy pictures about antiheroes, profanity-laden tirades against authority, or sexually explicit studies of flawed characters. At this point he could only be John Wayne, a nostalgic figure capable of sharing wisdom with the next generation or of updating

---
★
---

opposite WAYNE ON THE SET OF *THE COWBOYS* IN SANTA FE, NEW MEXICO, APRIL 1971. HIS BODY RUINED BY DECADES OF HARD WORK AND HARD LIVING, WAYNE SUFFERED INTENSE PAIN WHENEVER HE RODE A HORSE.

Wayne wanted fans to know what they were going to see before they settled into their seats. "Any roles have to be tailored to fit me," he remarked. "The big tough boy on the side of right—that's me. Simple themes. Save me from the nuances. I stay away from psychoanalyst's couch scenes." His audience deserved to be comfortable, he believed. That meant making Westerns, even if Wayne knew they weren't very good, and even if making them sapped his strength.

His body ached from a lifetime of scrapes, sprains, and breaks. Lung surgery and years of heavy smoking robbed him of breath. During the making of *Cahill, United States Marshal* (1972) he required a ladder to mount a horse. Good health seemed a thing of the past; he nursed broken ribs through *The Train Robbers* (1973), wrenched his knee while filming *Rooster Cogburn* (1975), and acquired an unshakeable cough that sometimes left him gasping for air.

For all his suffering, Wayne could still make a decent Western when he had the right script, director, and cast. The water rights battle that forms the central conflict in *Chisum* (1970) drove an entertaining character study of Billy the Kid (Geoffrey Deuel), future lawman Pat Garrett (Glenn Corbett), and rancher John Chisum (Wayne). In *Big Jake* (1971), Wayne plays Jacob McCandles, a toned-down version

traditions for modern audiences. Wayne's ageless mantra of taking care of your own business, of treating the other guy right unless he mistreats you, remained unchanged. In true Western tradition his characters kept aloof from social bonds such as marriage, family, and civilization. Despite this, they found ways to share their wisdom with young people, whether as the estranged husband and father of *Big Jake* (1970), the elderly rancher of *The Cowboys* (1972), or the grizzled cop of *Brannigan* (1975).

of Ethan Edwards, who evokes melancholy, humor, and self-mockery while searching for his kidnapped grandson. Out of place in an early twentieth-century world of motorcycles and telephones, McCandles endures constant amazement from people who thought he was long dead. He revels in his refusal to change with the times. McCandles even recalls, anachronistically, the golden age of Hollywood when he refers to a chest supposedly filled with money but actually crammed with newspaper as "the stuff that dreams are made of"—an inside joke for fans of 1941's *The Maltese Falcon*.

opposite ANN-MARGRET LAUGHING WITH WAYNE ON LOCATION FOR *THE TRAIN ROBBERS*, 1972. *above* DUKE DISCUSSES THE FILMING OF *CHISUM* WITH HIS SON AND EXECUTIVE PRODUCER MICHAEL WAYNE, 1970. A DISTANT FATHER DURING HIS EARLIER YEARS, WAYNE GREW CLOSER TO HIS CHILDREN AND GRANDCHILDREN AS HE AGED.

"You haven't changed, have you?" Big Jake's ex-wife asks. "Not one bit," he responds. Wayne, however, was feeling intense pressure to change. His fans still loved him, but there seemed to be fewer of them. Countercultural Westerns such as *Billy Jack* (1971), *McCabe & Mrs. Miller* (1971), and *Pat Garrett and Billy the Kid* (1973) turned big profits while Wayne's conventional entries struggled to break even.

With one eye on the burgeoning urban vigilante genre headlined by 1971's *Dirty Harry*—a part that Wayne turned down—and *The French Connection* (1971), Wayne relocated his character to the modern city. The resulting films, *McQ* (1974) and *Brannigan* (1975) were both critical and box-office flops. Try as he might, the aging, heavyset actor looked out of place in Seattle and London. His laconic "knock, knock" after bursting through a door and feeble efforts to dash through the streets were pale imitations of Eastwood and Hackman. "You're just so damned ... solid," a young British policewoman gushed in *Brannigan*. It was impossible, however, for Wayne to be solid when backed by a jazzy, funky soundtrack that combined elements of *Shaft*, Stax Records, and porno music.

Wayne had reached retirement age with no hopes of retiring. Besides loving his work, he was in no financial condition to quit making movies.

But everything was falling apart. Spiro Agnew and Richard Nixon, his political heroes, resigned from office in disgrace. His mother, Molly, died in 1970, her gut full of tumors. His brother, Bobby, died of throat cancer three months later. Stomach cancer got John Ford, the father of his cinematic family, in 1973. Pilar moved out of the house soon after. Wayne had already moved on, this time forming an emotional relationship with his young secretary, Pat Stacy.

He still had his children and grandchildren, who now became the center of his life. Duke regretted not spending more time with his kids from his

opposite WAYNE AT HOME WITH WIFE PILAR AND DAUGHTER MARISA, CIRCA 1969. *above* DUKE AT HOME WITH HIS SON ETHAN, CIRCA 1969. AS HE GREW OLDER, WAYNE DEDICATED HIMSELF TO BEING A MORE ENGAGED FATHER FOR HIS SECOND FAMILY THAN HE HAD FOR HIS OLDER CHILDREN.

marriage to Josie and resolved to make it up to Aissa, John Ethan, and Marisa. Movie sets became staging areas for family reunions. "Not only are his own children around," Maureen O'Hara laughed, "but any number of his grandchildren. For God's sake, there's never been a time that one, two, or three of them aren't crawling all over him." He could be a smothering parent at times, sniping whenever his teenagers chafed at his authority. At other times, however, Duke showed extraordinary patience and understanding during moments that would have caused "John Wayne" to spank their hides raw.

In a sure sign that his time had passed, Wayne became a popular recipient of awards and honors. USC granted him an honorary doctorate. *Photoplay* magazine gave him a Gold Medal commendation. The Marines presented him with an Iron Mike award. A George Washington Award from the Freedom Foundation, a Scopus Award from the Friends of Hebrew University, a Kindness to Animals award from the American Humane Association. The list went on and on. Everyone wanted a last moment with Wayne before he faded away.

Duke's fans expected him to be John Wayne at all times. In 1974, he rode an armored personnel carrier through a barrage of snowballs, most of them thrown in jest, into Cambridge, Massachusetts, to accept the Harvard *Lampoon*'s Brass Balls Award. Treating the subsequent mock press conference like a verbal shootout, he reveled in stunning his liberal enemies with perfectly timed put-downs. A student stood behind Wayne wearing a *True Grit*–style eye patch as the star fielded questions shouted from the floor. "Is it true that your toupee is real mohair?" one asked. "No sir, that's real hair. Not mine, but real hair," Wayne joked as the audience roared.

The "old warhorse," as CBS news called him, still had some fight even though his life and his career were winding down. After debacles like *Rooster Cogburn* (1975), an ill-advised *True Grit* sequel that paired Wayne with Katharine Hepburn, fans wondered whether it was time for their hero to be put to pasture. "Maybe one of our Bicentennial projects ought to be a search for a movie worthy of a national treasure like John Wayne," a *Time* magazine reviewer wrote in 1975, not long before Duke headed to Carson City, Nevada, to start work on *The Shootist*.

Glendon Swarthout's grim tale of a gunslinger suffering from rectal and prostate cancer struck Wayne as prime movie material. Its protagonist, J. B. Books, a Wild West character adrift in a modernizing world, was in many ways a man after Wayne's own heart. "The end of an era, the sunset, you might say. You're the sole survivor, Mr. Books,

---

BIG JAKE PROOF SHEET

Film proof sheet from behind the scenes with Wayne and his son on the set of *Big Jake*, 1971.

THE SHOOTIST PROOF SHEET

Film proof sheet from Wayne's last film *The Shootist*, 1976

opposite WAYNE WITH HIS SON, ETHAN, IN *BIG JAKE*, 1971.

and we're thankful for that," one reporter tells him. Like Wayne's film character, Books uses violence to resolve disputes and claims to have never shot someone who didn't deserve it.

Adapting the novel for the screen presented problems for Wayne, who clashed with director Don Siegel throughout the production. Books is no hero, rather a brutal man who revels in the mechanics of killing. As Swarthout described one of his shots: "The round was well placed. It entered the torso in the intercostal space between the ribs, missing the spine but mangling the paravertebral muscles, and exited by breaking out a wide swatch of the sternum … The aortic root had been transected, severed by the bullet … Blood sprayed from the outlet in his breast as though from the nozzle of a hose, drenching tables and chairs and tiles."

Books's young protégé, Gillom Rogers, presented another difficulty. Gillom, the son of the good-hearted widow and lodging house owner Bond Rogers, is a nasty piece of work, a greedy thief who can't wait for his mother's lodger to die so he can have Books's precious pistols for himself. It is Gillom who, following the climatic shootout, delivers the head shot that puts Books out of his misery. Killing the wounded man infuses him with "the sweet clean feel of being born." Swarthout therefore concluded that violence begat violence,

that death does not bring redemption.

As a film, *The Shootist* (1976) had greater moral complexity than most of Wayne's efforts, yet it muted the novel's more downbeat elements. Wayne is considerably more spry than his literary counterpart, whose cancer is often described in horrific detail. Unlike the novel, the movie casts Books as a former lawman who possesses a strict moral code. "I won't be wronged, I won't be insulted, I won't be laid a hand on," he tells Gillom (Ron Howard). "I don't do these things to other people, and I require the same from them." The cinematic Books does not stoop to shooting someone in the back, as happened in the novel.

Finally, the film reshapes Gillom from a hoodlum in training to a troubled youth who needs only a little paternal guidance of the sort that Wayne had specialized in over the past few years. This time around Gillom kills a bartender who fires two fatal shots into Books's ravaged body. With a look of disgust, Gillom hurls the gun away in an implicit renunciation of violence. Books looks on with tender eyes, silently nodding his approval as he slips into death's welcoming arms.

With this scene Wayne completes the mission he began forty-six years earlier with *The Big Trail*. The West has been tamed, lawlessness destroyed, and the next generation enlightened. There is no

longer any need for men like Books, no more than there is for a Breck Coleman or a Ringo Kid. Wayne's characters had traveled the same arc in dozens of films, sacrificing their way of life in order to bring progress to America. No longer, however, could that sacrifice be painless. Wayne no longer got the girl at the end, no longer settled down to a comfortable life as a rancher. He had given his life in the name of civilization before, in *The Man Who Shot Liberty Valance*, for example, but rarely so poignantly, or with such grace.

Critics cheered Wayne's performance. Audiences gave *The Shootist* a more tepid response, as it pulled in a mere $6 million in ticket sales, less than half of what Clint Eastwood's *The Outlaw Josey Wales* took in that same year. Movie fans saw it as a worthy if depressing addition to Wayne's oeuvre. No one then knew that it would be his last picture, that his nod to Gillom would be his final on-screen benediction. Those realities would later enhance *The Shootist*'s significance, transforming a very good movie into an extraordinarily moving one.

---

above RON HOWARD AS GILLOM ROGERS AND WAYNE IN *THE SHOOTIST*, 1976. AS HIS BODY SLOWLY BETRAYED HIM, WAYNE PULLED OUT ONE LAST REMARKABLE PERFORMANCE FOR THE CAMERA.

In retrospect, it is tempting to believe that Duke knew he was done, even though he simply couldn't have. The opening credits alone, which feature clips from his glory days—*Red River, Rio Bravo, Hondo*—today still cause a lump to rise in one's throat.

Duke did admit that he was in trouble. "There's no such thing as growing old gracefully," he told Pat Stacy. "It's all deterioration, decay." Recent bouts with pneumonia, influenza, and gallstones left him in bad condition even before filming began. After completing scenes, he rushed to his trailer to suck oxygen. An inner-ear infection and another case of influenza kept him off the shoot for two weeks. His persistent hacking ruined takes. Scenes with Jimmy Stewart, who played Doc Hostetler, proved especially difficult, as Stewart couldn't hear and Duke couldn't breathe. Wayne was bloated and was starting to have trouble urinating. A decade after his lung surgery, the "big C" still loomed large in his mind. "It's all so damn irritating," he fumed.

———————— ★ ————————

"Before we get to the big one," Bob Hope said before introducing the Best Picture Award at the 1978 Oscars, "here's a word for one of Hollywood's biggest ... We want you to know, Duke, we miss you tonight. We expect to see you amble out here in person next year, because nobody else can walk in John Wayne's boots."

It had been a tough two years. Wayne was too much of a medical liability for a movie producer to hire and too exhausted to produce his own picture. After *The Shootist*, he made a few commercials and mused about a comeback. But not even John Wayne could defeat time. As Hope spoke, Duke was in the hospital recovering from open-heart surgery, followed soon after by a case of hepatitis. Pounds slipped off his burly frame. Food tasted bad, even the spicy Mexican dishes and charbroiled steaks he loved so much.

Duke agreed to sit down with Barbara Walters a few days before entering UCLA medical center for exploratory surgery on his stomach. Not surprisingly, he was in an introspective mood. "I have a deep faith that there is a Supreme Being," he replied when asked about his philosophy of life. "The fact that He's let me stick around a little longer, or She's let me stick around a little longer, certainly goes great with me, and I want to hang around as long as I'm healthy and not in anybody's way."

"Has it been a good life?" she asked.

"Great for me."

Two days later doctors removed John Wayne's stomach. It was riddled with cancerous tumors, just

like John Ford's had been, and just like his mother's had been. Subsequent tests indicated that the surgery came too late; Wayne's lymph nodes were shot full of growths. Doctors could try radiation and more experimental treatments but had little hope of arresting the spread.

Like J. B. Books, Wayne was determined to ride off on his own terms. That meant meeting Bob Hope's challenge by presenting the Best Picture Award at the 1979 Oscars. He was weak and emaciated by that April. His face was wasted, its skin

flabby. His back screamed constantly. The new tuxedo he bought for the occasion was already too big for him. But he was going.

Host Johnny Carson gave Duke a suitable introduction, calling him "an American institution" and cuing up Hope's message of the previous year. Then he spoke words never to be heard on television again: "Ladies and gentlemen, Mr. John Wayne."

The crowd leapt to its feet as Duke sauntered down one of the spiral staircases flanking the

above BARBARA WALTERS INTERVIEWING WAYNE IN 1979. ALTHOUGH CANCER WAS RAVAGING HIS BODY, WAYNE INSISTED THAT HE WAS OPTIMISTIC FOR THE FUTURE.

stage. He absorbed the applause as if knowing he would never hear it again. There was no showboating on his part, but rather real gratitude. Clasping his hands nervously at the waist—those hands, which he finally got under control back in the mid-1930s—he smiled graciously as he rocked from side to side, nodding to the crowd. Then a brief shake of the head, an ambiguous gesture indicating either his inability to process the moment or his conviction that it was time to get on with it.

A billion television viewers heard that voice. It was thin, gravelly, hollow, but it was definitely *that* voice. "That's just about the only medicine a fellow'd ever need," Wayne croaked. After observing that both he and Oscar got their start in Hollywood in 1928, he delivered a final piece of bravado before turning to business. "We're both a little weather beaten," he observed, "but we're still here and plan to be around a whole lot longer." Two months later, on June 11, 1979, he was gone.

──────────── ✮ ────────────

"I never *really* thought Duke could die," director Andrew McLaglen said. Wayne was supposed to be the invincible hero, as permanent as the buttes of Monument Valley.

And perhaps he really is invincible. His immortality rests upon the great pillars he left behind, the two hundred cinematic monuments to a way of life that seems quaintly outdated, yet holds tremendous appeal for everyone who believes that an individual should treat others right and demand the same in return. John Wayne has become more than a hero, more than an icon. He embodies a rite of passage, a ritual repeated whenever a parent sits down with his child and says, "Watch this movie with me." Wayne is more ubiquitous than ever. His movies appear on a dozen channels. His talk and his walk are imitated. His image appears in bars around the world. For many living in the twenty-first century, he *is* America.

Duke would have no patience for such rhapsodizing. "God, how I hate solemn funerals," he once remarked. "When I die, take me into a room and burn me. Then my family and a few good friends should get together, have a few good belts and talk about the crazy old times we all had together." When asked how he wanted to be remembered he replied, "Feo, fuerte y formal," Spanish for "ugly, strong, and dignified." Correct on two of three counts, to be sure.

At another time he offered what seems a more fitting epitaph: "Damn, I'm the stuff men are made of!"

──────────── ✮ ────────────

DEDICATION

To John Wayne, who gave us almost 200 movies, and to the millions of fans who walked the walk, talked the talk, and wished, for one moment, they had faced down the Plummer brothers on that dark street in Lordsburg.

ACKNOWLEDGMENTS

The authors would like to thank the fine crew at becker&meyer!, especially Amelia Riedler and Dana Youlin, who shepherded this project to completion with grace, humor, and patience.

ABOUT THE AUTHORS

Randy Roberts has received four Pulitzer Prize nominations, for his books *John Wayne: American*, *Jack Dempsey: The Manassa Mauler*, *Papa Jack: Jack Johnson and the Era of White Hopes*, and *Joe Louis: Hard Times Man*. His most recent book is *A Team for America: The Army-Navy Game That Rallied a Nation*. He is also the author of *A Line in the Sand: The Alamo in Blood and Memory* and many other books on American history. He served as a consultant for the Emmy-winning Ken Burns documentary "Unforgivable Blackness: The Rise and Fall of Jack Johnson," and has also consulted for the History Channel. Roberts is a Distinguished Professor of History at Purdue University in Indiana.

David Welky is the author of several books, including *The Moguls and the Dictators: Hollywood and the Coming of World War II*, *The Thousand-Year Flood: The Ohio-Mississippi Disaster of 1937*, and *Everything Was Better in America: Print Culture in the Great Depression*. He has also published studies of John Ford, football, and late-nineteenth-century masculinity. Welky is an associate professor of history at the University of Central Arkansas.

IMAGE CREDITS

Front cover: © Sunset Boulevard/Corbis

Page 2: Courtesy Everett Collection

Page 5: © 20th Century Fox Film Corporation/Courtesy Everett Collection

Page 6: Michael Ochs Archives/Getty Images

Page 9: Hulton Archive/Getty Images

Page 11: Pictorial Parade/Getty Images

Page 11 (yearbook): Courtesy of Joe Zuckschwerdt

Page 12: Southern California/Collegiate Images/Getty Images

Page 15: John Kobal Foundation/Getty Images

Page 16: Courtesy Everett Collection

Page 19: Mary Evans/Ronald Grant/Courtesy Everett Collection

Page 20: © 20th Century Fox Film Corporation/Courtesy Everett Collection

Page 21: © John Springer Collection/Corbis

Page 22: © 20th Century Fox Film Corporation/Courtesy Everett Collection

Page 23: © 20th Century Fox Film Corporation/Courtesy Everett Collection

Page 24: © John Springer Collection/Corbis

Page 27: Courtesy Everett Collection

Page 28: Courtesy Everett Collection

Page 30: © Bettmann/Corbis

Page 31: Courtesy Everett Collection

Page 32: Courtesy Everett Collection

Page 33: Courtesy Everett Collection

Page 35: Courtesy Everett Collection

Page 36: Courtesy Everett Collection

Page 39: John Kobal Foundation/Getty Images

Page 40: © Sunset Boulevard/Corbis

Page 43: © 20th Century Fox Film Corporation/Courtesy Everett Collection

Page 45: United Artists/The Kobal Collection

Page 47: © 20th Century Fox Film Corporation/Courtesy Everett Collection

Page 49: © Bettmann/Corbis

Page 49 (poster): Courtesy Everett Collection

Page 49 (ad): Mary Evans/Ronald Grant/Courtesy Everett Collection

Page 50 (poster): Courtesy Everett Collection

Page 50 (ad): Mary Evans/Ronald Grant/Courtesy Everett Collection

Page 51: Courtesy Everett Collection

Page 52: United Artists/The Kobal Collection

Page 53: © 20th Century Fox Film Corporation/Courtesy Everett Collection

Page 54: United Artists/The Kobal Collection

Page 56: Courtesy Everett Collection

Page 58: Republic/The Kobal Collection

Page 61: Courtesy Everett Collection

Page 63: Michael Ochs Archives/Getty Images

Page 64: Courtesy Everett Collection

Page 66: Courtesy Everett Collection

Page 67: Courtesy Everett Collection

Page 69: Courtesy Everett Collection

Page 70: Michael Ochs Archives/Getty Images

Page 71: Courtesy Everett Collection

Page 72: Courtesy Everett Collection

Page 73: © John Springer Collection/Corbis

Page 74: © Sunset Boulevard/Corbis

Page 77: Courtesy Everett Collection

Page 78: © Corbis

Page 81: Courtesy Everett Collection

Page 82 (application): Courtesy National Archives

Page 82 (poster): Courtesy Everett Collection

Page 83: Courtesy Everett Collection

Page 83 (poster): Courtesy Everett Collection